# GOD AND FOUNDERS' REMEDY FOR AMERICA

Stephen G. Forfer, B.S. MDIV

silvanus

publishing, inc.

# Disclaimer

GOD AND FOUNDERS' REMEDY FOR AMERICA
Cover Design created by Silvanus Publishing, Inc.
All biblical quotes are taken from The King James Holy Bible
(Charles of the Scottish James Family).
Typography by Silvanus Publishing, Inc.
Copyright © 2015 by Silvanus Publishing, Inc.
Published by Silvanus Publishing, Inc.
www.silvanuspublishing.com

Forfer, Stephen B.S. MDIV – GOD AND FOUNDERS'
REMEDY FOR AMERICA
by Stephen Forfer
146 pages
ISBN: 978-0-9969165-9-2
1. Religion. 2. Elite (Social Sciences)—United States. 3. United
States—Social Policy.

# TABLE OF CONTENTS

# Introduction

As a grateful son of a United States Naval Academy Veteran, I was gloriously saved in 1982 at the age of 25, as the motivation for this work comes from personal experience, observations and study of America's churches and nation, and most importantly Jesus the Bridegroom's Holy standards for His Bride as revealed in His inspired Word, the Bible!

Born and raised in the "Sin City of Bourbon Street" (New Orleans, Louisiana), my upbringing nonetheless greatly resembled the golden age of television's "Leave it to Beaver"!

We were a typical "Boomer" family of the 50's and 60's with devoted parents from the World War II generation who had endured many personal and national hardships, divinely compelling them to patriotically unite together to respect many time honored traditions, while understandably longing for a better life for their children!

My earliest and most vivid life-changing childhood memory occurred as a six year old in 1963, sitting on the living room floor playing as my mother watched the noon-time news report that apparently declared something about "School Prayer". Though too young and naive to grasp its consequences, mom was unaware I had noticed her tears! That night as she tucked me in for bed-time prayer, I curiously asked her "Why were you crying"?

Her response was the seed God planted that would help bring me to Christ and later call me to ministry as she sadly answered in my paraphrased recollection, "Because our nation is moving further and further away from God"!

Church attendance was a systematic part of our life growing up, something we faithfully did most Sundays unless Mardi Gras parades, ballgames, fishing trips or other recreational activities at times rendered us too weary to get up on Sunday mornings!

My church memories in the 60's included the family's thirty minute ride home hearing mom and dad lamenting over the above mentioned Supreme Court decision and many other "disturbing national trends", though at home we only prayed before meals or bed-time, and usually read the Bible only at Christmas and Easter.

I cherished being with my beloved father and his friends between Sunday School and Church service, listening to routine discussions of their military experiences, job promotions and raises, bigger houses and material acquisitions, ballgames and hobbies as they enjoyed their Winstons and Salems.

Church members showed proper respect to "the Reverend", who each Sunday in pulpit would tell us pleasant stories related to "God and heaven" (though I honestly cannot recall warnings about a real spiritual enemy or possibility of hell) that seemed to appease the slowly dwindling congregation.

To this youngster, "the church" seemed to be good, hard-working, fun-loving, fairly "patriotic and religious" people merely pursuing the good life. History reveals however that spiritually for any nation, the only thing necessary for evil to prevail is for good men to do nothing, as our Founders declared "Political slavery is ever preceded by sleep"!

In His Matthew 13 parable Jesus put it this way, "The kingdom of heaven is likened unto a man which sowed good seed in his field: But while men slept, his enemy came and sowed tares among the wheat, and went his way" (Matthew 13:24-25).

In recent decades America has reaped many unprecedented national spiritual plagues, as her churches slowly and subtly fell into a deep sleep, prompting an alarming disclaimer!

Though I earnestly pray these pages could, amidst her church's apathy and slumber coinciding with many New Testament warnings of the perilous last days, I am not so naïve to presume that this writing will "necessarily" succeed in waking up America's "sleeping giant" to the escalating moral and spiritual depravity our nation and world has prophetically only begun to experience!

So you may logically ask, "Then why bother trying if uncertain whether it will succeed in changing anything"?

Many Old Testament prophets were faced with this same dilemma, being called by God to warn sinners of His eternal judgment for their unrepentant wicked living, despite the likelihood that the vast majority would not repent regardless of their faithful prophetic warnings!

So why did these godly prophets set themselves up for almost certain persecution by proclaiming God's truth and redemptively exposing the sins of His people? The chilling answer to this question is unveiled in God's charge to His faithful prophet Ezekiel:

> "Son of man, I have made thee a WATCHMAN unto the house of Israel: therefore hear the word at my mouth, and give them warning from me – When I say unto the wicked, Thou shalt surely die; and thou givest him not warning… to save his life; the same wicked man shall die in his iniquity; but his blood will I require at thine hand – Yet if thou warn the wicked, and he turn not from his wickedness… he shall die in his iniquity; but thou hast delivered thy soul" (Ezekiel 3:17-19).

God's call to Ezekiel as a "watchman" carries virtually the same meaning as a New Testament word found in I Timothy 3:1 ("bishop", = overseer) which Paul used interchangeably with "pastor-elder" to describe His under-shepherd's God-given responsibility to spiritually lead, protect, warn and watch over the flock of Israel.

According to God, if His watchman was faithful to warn the wicked of their impending eternal destiny in their unrepentance, the watchman's hands would be absolved of any responsibility for their eternal peril!

But if God's watchman failed to give them warning and the wicked perished in their sin, the watchman himself would one day stand before God at His Bema Seat with hands stained by their blood, required to give account!

Though the true prophets of old shared a godliness and calling divinely distinctive and essential for the time and circumstances in which they lived to proclaim God's warnings of impending judgment, with many paying the ultimate price of martyrdom for their faith and obedience, this same God who never changes (Hebrews 13:8) is still able to raise His prophetic voice through seemingly insignificant but boldly redemptive earthly vessels today!

May America hear and heed His 4-R's REMEDY VISION before everlasting too late:

"Ye see the distress that we are in; COME, and let us (spiritually RESTORE)…that we be no more a reproach" (Nehemiah 2:17)!

## Chapter One

AMERICA'S ROOT PROBLEMS:

Prophetically Passive
"People-Pleaser" Pastors

Most of America today, from conservative Republicans and even liberal democrats can usually agree on one thing – our nation is beset with many intense problems in virtually every spectrum including political, social, economic, health, emotional and especially spiritual realms! But mortal opinions greatly vary on how to remedy them (see "God and Founders' 4-R's REMEDY VISION for America")!

But as we are going to see especially amidst the past several generations in America, it is Biblically evident that America's collective churches and particularly pastors bear primary responsibility in God's eyes, since as leadership goes, so go the rest!

Now it must first be confided that our intent is surely not to unjustly indict God's beloved remnant of prophetic pastors who faithfully proclaim truth and confront sin for the purpose of redemption no matter how unpopular it may be! But even this faithful remnant of pastors and leaders must be willing to Biblically embrace their shared responsibility for America's present spiritual condition even as Ezra and Nehemiah did for sinful Israel amidst and following her "Babylonian Captivity" (Jeremiah 24:1)!

But God is especially referring to today's many pastors who are actually a fulfillment of God's prophetic warnings: "Many false prophets shall rise, and shall deceive many" (Matthew 24:11) and "Do I seek to please God or men, for if I pleased men, I should not be the servant of Christ" (Galatians 1:10).

The many false prophets, religions and cults today preaching some "other gospel" than the Bible, from Mormonism to Muslim and from Jim Jones to Obama Bin Laden, are clearly evidenced, well documented and should be easily recognized in America's uniquely spiritual foundation (see "RE-DISCOVERING America's Republic")!

So for purposes of this writing under His Holy Spirit's prayerful guidance through His Word, we will primarily focus on the devastating "worldly conformities" occurring even within America's so-called "Christian" denominations by many prophetically passive "people-pleaser" pastors today! But why does God single out pastors as the primary problem? After all, the Bible teaches "For ALL have sinned and come short of the glory of God" (Romans 3:23) - so aren't we all guilty and share responsibility for the consequences of sin in our nation and world?

Of course, but as we will see God collectively holds pastors (and secondly church congregations!) primarily responsible for America's spiritual condition today!

Now I have a personal confession to make - I happen to be a former-pastor whom God subsequently called to the ministry of evangelism! So I speak from pastoral experience not as some holier than thou self-righteous saint of God, but as an imperfect and wretched but repentant sinner for whom Jesus died and rose again to save us from hell and provide victory over sin in order to daily conform us to Himself!

Now before posing the question I Biblically believe God is asking America's churches and especially pastors today, I am also compelled to assure Christian readers that as a blood-bought, born-again, Bible-based, baptized by immersion believer in Christ, I deeply love, support and faithfully endeavor to serve God's remnant churches who actively strive for holy living and Spirit-anointed witness to a lost and dying world!

Since the "Birthday of His Church" in Acts 2, God has always had and used a remnant of His people refusing to conform to the ways of an unrepentant lost world, divinely choosing to "come out from among them, and be ye separate, and touch not the unclean thing" (2 Corinthians 6:17)!

So the purpose of this book is surely not to disrespect God's true churches and leaders regardless of our spiritual condition, "For God so loved the world, that He gave His only begotten Son, that whosoever believeth in Him should not perish, but have ever-lasting life" (John 3:16), as she is still Biblically His bride for whom He gave His very life, evidencing His "agape" (unconditional) love for all people, including His covenant people Israel and His Bride the church regardless of our response to Him!

However, amidst the spiritual condition of many pastors and churches in America today, it is evident that God's purpose is to redemptively but righteously rebuke the widespread apathy, hypocrisy, carnal lifestyles, disobedience and worldly compromise of today's many pro-

3

fessing Christians, churches and pastors who assume God's unconditional love assures them forgiveness, failing to balance His unconditional love with His conditional forgiveness as the "Supreme Judge of the world" (Declaration of Independence)!

God's mercifully unconditional love never negates His conditional forgiveness dependent on our willingness to truly repent (turn) from our sin, as Jesus' first ministry message was "Repent, for the kingdom of heaven is at hand" (Matthew 4:17).

The Bible says, "If we confess our sins, He is faithful and just to forgive us our sins, and to cleanse us from all unrighteousness. If we say that we have not sinned, we make Him a liar, and His truth is not in us" (I John 1:9-10)!

Since God's churches are the Biblical barometer for the spiritual condition of nations, and since leadership inevitably influences its followers, amidst America's growing moral and spiritual bankruptcy especially during the past half century or more, this Holy God is no doubt prophetically grieved and angry with His Bride in America today!

A nation historically known for her rich Biblical heritage and faith bestowed by her Founders, America and many of her churches now tragically find herself lulled into a subtle but deep sleep. The foundations which once made her great continue to crumble under the pounding of our own carnality, with most of God's pastors and churches remaining passively silent with her head in the sand or actively contributing to our own demise!

Thus the Psalmist asks, "If the foundations be destroyed, what can the righteous do" (Psalm 11:3)? But God assures "The Lord is (still) in His holy temple…His eyes behold the children of men" (Psalm 11:4).

Make no mistake, this Omniscient (all-knowing) Heavenly Father obviously knew this peril would happen and is not the least bit surprised, as Paul warned "This know also, that in the last days perilous times shall come, for men shall be lovers of their own selves…lovers of pleasures more than lovers of God…For the time will come when they will not endure sound doctrine…and they shall turn away their ears from the truth" (2 Timothy 3:1-2, 4:3-4).

But the primary peril of our day is not the vile depravity of our now largely lost liberal nation with all her spiritual wickedness and reprobate living, for the spiritually lost are only doing what is natural for those who are "of (their) father the devil" to do (John 8:44).

No, for America the primary peril of these last days is that most of her churches in a nation historically blessed with a deeply rich spiritual heritage by her Founders now often contribute to our national peril via passive slumber or active carnality, as God says "unto whomsoever much is given, of him shall much be required" (Luke 12:48).

Many of today's church pastors and leaders have chosen the temporal rewards and earthly "ministry success" that comes from pleasing people over willingness to wait for the eternal heavenly rewards that come from pleasing God!

A secondary peril of these last days is that some of America's pastors and churches have even largely rationalized that since this last day peril is prophetically inevitable, there is nothing we can do about it so just relax, enjoy life and "go with the flow" as the peril takes its destructive course – or as the saying goes "If you can't beat them, join them" (see "Spiritually Asleep Sin-thetic Sheep")!

Consequently today in America, her once strong churches are often plagued by many of the same sin plagues prevalent in the lost world like apathy, slumber, pride, rebellion, adultery, divorce, unwed pregnancy, alcohol, tobacco, drugs, greed, gambling, dishonesty, division and abortion just to name a few, even remaining largely silent on sodomy (Bible term for "homosexual or same-sex" implying God's judgment - Genesis 19), as most of these sins are becoming almost as common within many of God's so-called churches as outside! Instead of the world becoming more like the church through her Christ-like witness and lifestyle, with few exceptions it seems America's churches have sadly and sordidly become more like the lost world!

Such was often the case with God's chosen people Israel throughout Scripture, prompting God to painfully remind His covenant people that their own wicked living was the real reason for their nation's condition and judgment as He declared, "If MY people, which are called by My name, shall humble themselves and pray, and seek my face, and turn from their wicked ways, then will I hear from heaven, and will forgive their sin, and will heal their land" (2 Chronicles 7:14). Many church members today often deflect these prophetic last day warnings, pointing to "those wicked politicians" or organizations like the "American Civil Liberties Union" (ACLU) and "Americans United for the Separation of Church and State", concluding "If THEY would just repent and get right with God, America would be okay"! But as has always been the case throughout history to this day, God declares that

"Judgment must begin at the house of God, and if it first begin at us, what shall the end be of them that obey not the gospel of God" (I Peter 4:17)?

Wicked rulers are merely a divinely allowed judgment for the wicked living of God's own people! This natural pattern of excuses and blame-shifting for our sinful condition can be traced throughout human existence dating back to the Garden of Eden, when God told Adam and Eve they could enjoy the fruit of all the trees in the garden except one!

We know what happened - they tragically chose to disobey God, and the consequence of sin has marred our earthly existence ever since until Jesus triumphantly returns to rapture His true beloved Bride!

Ever since Adam, we sinful human beings have had to daily endure the devastating consequences of our decision. But perhaps the most profound irony about a Holy God toward sin in the Genesis 3 account is that though divinely and deeply grieved, He was ultimately not only grieved that we sinned as devastating as that was omnisciently knowing we would, but was also grieved with Adam's response to Him in his fallen state.

In Genesis 3:9, the Lord first seeks and calls out to a hiding Adam (not Eve!), evidencing the man's primary responsibility and accountability for their sin due to God's creative order and function assigned to him (Genesis 2:5,7).

God's account even reveals that Adam was "with her" (passively allowed her sin – Genesis 3:6) even before he himself ate of the forbidden fruit!

But notice Adam's response to God – "The woman whom thou gavest to be with me, she gave me of the tree, and I did eat" (Genesis 3:12)! In other words, "It was her fault, not mine"! And since the woman was given to Adam by God in the first place, he even blames God! Thus the man not only passively committed the first sin in human history, but was personally guilty of the first attempted cover-up!

Surely the woman would answer more responsibly since Adam had already blamed her and God, so there wasn't anyone else left to blame, right? But in Genesis 3:13 she responds, "The serpent beguiled me, and I did eat". In other words, "The devil made me do it" as comedian Flip Wilson used to light-heartedly joke - sound familiar?

Because of their unrepentant response before God, the downward spiral of sin's consequences was able to gather momentum on its destructive path, when these consequences could have been redemptively forgiven and His spiritual healing begun by their simple and proper response of repentance and faith in God!

The good news is, even the destructive nature of sin no longer has to have personal "dominion" (control) over us because of the finished work of the Lord Jesus Christ on Calvary's cross 2,000 years ago, as Romans 6:14 offers Christ's true followers "For sin shall not have dominion over you" as we by faith personally receive Christ and begin to obey Him! Thus the Bridegroom, the Lord Jesus Christ "loved the church and gave Himself for it; that He might sanctify and cleanse it with the washing of water (Jesus the Living Water) by the Word, that He might present it to Himself a glorious church, not having spot, or wrinkle, or any such thing; but that it should be holy and without blemish" (Ephesians 5:25-27).
The sinless Bridegroom would not settle for anything less than a purely spotless and Holy Bride!

His salvation and subsequent sanctification process begins the moment we genuinely pray the spiritual "A-B-C's": Admit we're a sinner – "For all have sinned and come short of the glory of God" (even Billy Graham and the Pope - Romans 3:23) - Repent (turn from our sin) and Believe on the Lord Jesus Christ (Romans 10:9) - and Commit our life to obediently follow Christ – "If ye love me, keep my commandments" (John 14:15)!

But if salvation is this simple, then why do we as His Bride the church often "continue in sin" and passively often allow it to "reign" in our mortal bodies" (Romans 6:1,12)? Who is primarily at fault in God's eyes? After all, don't we need someone to blame?

The key word to God is primarily. Though each of us obviously bears personal primary accountability for the sin we bring to our own individual lives, God Biblically holds pastors primarily accountable for what goes on within His local churches!

We should not be surprised, since leadership is the key to any family, church, organization or nation! Now I surely realize the awkwardness of indicting my own ministry calling, some of whom God surely commends as genuine godly men of the cross of Christ!

Praise God for this remaining remnant of God's under-shepherds who even today still have the courage and conviction to strive to live consecrated lives, proclaiming truth and boldly but redemptively confronting sin no matter the personal cost to them, their families or their ministry security and success!

But it is divinely evident that the root reason why most of our churches today have become so "sin tolerant" is because many pastors and leaders have become prophetically sin tolerant, often valuing job status and security more than faithfully striving to keep Jesus' bride pure and clean from sin.

When a man heeds God's divine call to ministry, each will accountably answer for himself a critical question which will inevitably reveal his ultimate excellence or failure in God's eyes at His Bema Seat (or perhaps even Great White throne) on judgment day:

"Am I willing to passively allow even a little sin to leaven (defile) Christ's Bride in order to retain my position"?

Consider, if all of today's pastors were the genuinely godly men He requires, how can so many pastors and leaders comfortably and successfully co-exist in America's many ungodly sin-infested churches today?

Jesus could not, as he lasted only five prophetically short and spiritually hostile days from Palm Sunday to Good Friday among Jerusalem's persecuting Pharisees before being politically but voluntarily and only temporarily "terminated"!

Cross-denominationally today, it is statistically evident that forced terminations of even godly remnant pastors are increasing, as this remnant of godly men are being persecuted and often expelled by today's spiritually lukewarm or dead churches for taking a bold stand against her worldly and apathetic lifestyles.

Praise God for such courageous Christ-like men, as Jesus exhorts "Blessed are ye when men shall hate you and shall separate you from their company and cast out your name as evil for the Son of man's sake – Rejoice ye in that day, for behold, your reward is great in heaven" (Luke 6:22-23).

However based on today's epidemic of publicly documented cases, it is also apparent that the increasing moral and doctrinal failures of many pastors influencing our nation's moral and spiritual decline also accounts for much of this rise in forced pastor terminations, sadly often Biblically disqualifying such church leaders from ministry.

Obviously sin's presence is felt in every church within both ministry and laity, otherwise she would be perfect, and we know there are not and never will be any perfect earthly churches or people around! As my godly former pastor and continued spiritual mentor often fittingly warned, "If you ever find a perfect church, don't join it as you'll ruin it" – how true for all of us!

But scripture reveals that God holds His divinely called pastors to an even higher moral and spiritual standard, as Paul charges "A bishop (overseer-pastor) then must be blameless (above reproach of men)…vigilant, sober, of good behavior…not a novice, lest being lifted up with pride he fall into the condemnation of the devil" (I Timothy 3:2-6).

As previously mentioned, Jesus reveals the reason for His lofty spiritual requirements especially for church pastors, declaring "For unto whomsoever much is given, of him shall much be required" (Luke 12:48). Since the quality of leadership is the key influence on followers in any spectrum of life, Jesus especially requires much from His under-shepherds of His flock!

In God's infinite wisdom, He knew that leadership greatly influences followers! Thus in His church, God divinely charges His pastors with ultimate earthly responsibility, then justly and appropriately balances pastors with Biblical authority to lead His sheep in the ways of the Great Shepherd through His Word!

Remember Christ's commitment to His Bride - to "present it to Himself a glorious church, not having spot, or wrinkle, or any such thing, but that it should be holy and without blemish".

12

Remember that in the Garden of Eden God was not only concerned about Adam's sin, also his response to Him in his fallen state!

The root problem within spiritual leadership today is passive toleration of unrepentant sin within God's church. Many pastors daily witness blatant sin and disobedience to Christ in His church, but simply passively turn their heads because we have apparently grown accustomed to accepting the bride's many "little imperfections" no matter how harmful or destructive they may be, fearing consequences for taking a stand!

Collectively pastors have largely forsaken our commitment to strive to keep the bride pure and unspotted from sin in practice as well as by position in Christ, as Paul aptly warns even "a little leaven leaveneth the whole lump" (I Corinthians 5:6).

The truth is, most pastors today have passively accepted the philosophy that we simply must tolerate some sin in the church, because to issue a call for absolute perfection would obviously be an unrealistic, unattainable and self-defeating goal - after all, nobody's perfect!

This is the primary evidence of critical compromise by many prophetically passive "people-pleaser" pastors in America's churches today!

In Matthew 5:48, Jesus issues to His church an apparently "unattainable impossible" challenge "Be ye therefore perfect, even as your Father which is in heaven is perfect". How ridiculous and futile this seems! Does Jesus really expect even saved sinners to achieve the same sinless perfection in our earthly lives that He modeled in His?

13

Thankfully the word "perfect" here does not mean "without sin", but rather translates "to be mature or complete in God",[1] which divinely aids our understanding of His goal for us. But what likely saddens the heart of God most toward pastors and churches today is that many of us tend to become quite comfortable and content with our under-achieving state of spiritual lostness or maturation without ever even attempting to strive for Jesus' sinless perfection because of its perceived impossibility!

So we usually give up and resign in defeat before ever trying for Jesus' perfection. But remember, God is not as concerned if we fall short of His perfect standard since He knows we surely will, but that we genuinely strive for it as evidenced by our repentant response to our failures and sins!

On a daily basis, do we actually come to Him in genuine repentance, honestly striving with all our heart to "press toward the mark" (Philippians 3:14), or do we simply continue asking (or even fail to ask) forgiveness for the same repetitious sins because we have systematically given up in defeat, which leads us to perpetually "continue in sin that grace may abound" (Romans 6:1)?

In His infinite wisdom, God refused to compromise or lower His perfect sinless standard to accommodate mortal men, knowing that to strive for anything less than perfection would only serve to inevitably sentence us to wider margins of failure and despair, for at whatever height the spiritual bar is set, human nature and accomplishment is conditioned by sin to "come SHORT of the mark" (Romans 3:23)

This explains why Jesus chose to charge His church with His seemingly unattainable perfect standard to strive for, though He knew in practice we would never fully reach it here on earth, instead of giving us an easier and more mortally attainable but unworthy goal, since the Father's dedication is to "conform us to the (very) image of His Son" (Romans 8:29)!

When Jesus' true Bride the church collectively joins her Bridegroom in glory at His Rapture, she will be "without blemish" in practice as well as positionally in Christ!

But perhaps the divine importance of at least striving for earthly perfection is best illustrated in the realm of sports and athletic competition, a personal favorite subject of mine since childhood and often used by the Apostle Paul to illustrate spiritual truths, given his Greek audience's intense love of athletic competition!

You have heard the old saying "Records are made to be broken"! This is obviously true throughout the nostalgic history of sports, but why is this so?

In 1976, Olympian Nadia Comenici of Romania became the first and only gymnast to ever achieve a "perfect ten" in the history of the sport, though expert subsequent scrutiny of her stunning performance reveals a "microscopic" imperfection or two!

Though no competitor in prior history had ever achieved a perfect score, year after year this fact did nothing to stop the many determined, courageous and highly-dedicated athletes from striving with everything they had to achieve perfection, knowing if perfection was their goal, the closer they would likely come to it and thus more likely to win the gold, even if with a slightly less than perfect score!

But what if gymnastic officials had arbitrarily determined prior to 1976 that "since a perfect ten is unrealistic, unattainable and therefore self-defeating, we will officially lower the ultimate standard of competition to a mere nine and one half"!

Obviously Nadia or any other competitor would have never achieved a perfect ten, since their ultimate goal to strive for would have been reduced to a lower and unworthy target - as the old saying goes "If you don't have a target, you'll never hit it"!

In 1968, American long-jumper and "former" world record holder Bob Beamon set what most experts considered to be the most amazing and perhaps unbreakable record in sports history by soaring twenty nine feet two and one half inches, breaking fellow-American Ralph Boston's old record by almost two feet in a sport where mere inches or even fractions of inches usually separate the competitors!

Legendary sports journalist Dick Schaap even wrote a book about Beamon's incredible landmark leap entitled, "The Perfect Jump"!

Some sports officials even predicted nobody would ever surpass Beamon's freakish new standard, given the tremendous margin by which he had soared to exceed the old record. But finally in 1991, fellow-American Mike Powell did the seemingly impossible, surpassing even this apparently "perfect" standard!

But though it took almost a quarter-century to surpass this lofty and seemingly impossible record, it did not stop countless determined athletes over the years from continuing to strive for it until someone finally broke it!

But what would have happened if track officials in 1968 had presumed, "Since no mortal athlete can possibly attain this unreachable standard, we will just ignore Beamon's mark and continue to recognize the old record as the official and more attainable standard to shoot for"!

Powell's accomplishment would never have been set in motion, since at whatever height the bar is set, sinful human nature is pre-conditioned to generally under-achieve!

But in spite of the perpetual presence of sin in our lives which has rendered our human existence grossly flawed and imperfect, thankfully since God created us in His perfect image there still remains deep within the soul of humanity an undeniably genuine longing for a divinely higher plane of existence than the one we are otherwise limited to, which is precisely the reason Jesus came to redeem us and establish His church!

This would even explain why the most accomplished people and athletes are not always blessed with the greatest raw talent, but are intensely motivated both inwardly and by their wise mentors or coaches to achieve the highest standard of perfection!

But even many highly talented athletes who settle for the tutelage of passive coaches who fail to challenge them with perfection perhaps because of their own personal failures or grossly underestimated perceptions of his athlete's capabilities, usually only perform to the level of the inferior standard the athlete perceives his coach truly believes he is capable of achieving!

Tragically, this is what many prophetically passive people-pleaser pastors have done in spiritually overseeing Christ's church – passively and perpetually allowing the perfect standard of Christ to be lowered in attempt to accommodate our own flawed perceptions of congregations' spiritual potential, and the results have been devastating since human spiritual growth and development is pre-conditioned by sin to under-achieve the targeted standard!

Fearing persecution by the flock and loss of position for insisting on striving for the perfect and sinless standard of Christ, prophetic people-pleaser pastors passively allow His precious bride to be defiled and blemished with a vast arsenal of "little sins not important enough to lose their position over"!

The common explanation for this chronic passivity is, "Don't rock the boat", which by human logic appears legitimate, especially if a prospective pastor did not transparently confide his prayerful intention to redemptively but boldly confront sin by authority of the Word in order to preserve the spiritual purity of Christ's Bride!

This is the root reason many pastors today are a fulfillment of apocalyptic prophecy - because they are usually filled with fear instead of braced with boldness! For lack of a more discreet way to put it, many have a "wet noodle for a backbone" as the saying goes, which Biblically reveals their lack of spiritual courage to redemptively confront sin within God's church.

The God of the Bible knew that the "fear of man" is of
ultimate danger to His under-shepherds and church, because fear will ultimately overtake a man and cause

him to concede defeat before even trying rather than stand up to the enemy!

It was fear for his own life which caused Peter to deny Jesus, and fear which caused all of Jesus' own disciples except John to scatter and abandon Him at His crucifixion. Any time we are fearful of men or circumstances even within the church, we can be sure this fear did not come from God, as Paul reminds "God hath not given us the spirit of fear, but of power, and of love, and of a sound mind" (2 Timothy 1:7).

This fear of man which weakens and defeats so many pastors and churches is actually evidence that we really do not love and trust God as we ought, since "there is no fear in love, but perfect love casteth out fear" (I John 4:18).

God assures His true under-shepherds and sheep "I will never leave thee nor forsake thee – so that we may boldly say, the Lord is my helper, and I will not fear what man shall do unto me" (Hebrews 13:5-6).

In 2 Corinthians 11:23-27, Paul recounts the many shipwrecks and perils, oppositions, beatings and imprisonments he faced for the cause of Christ. But in Romans 8:31 he boldly and triumphantly declares "If God be for us, who can be against us"?

Acts 4:13 documents one of the most contrastingly powerful personal transformations of one of Jesus' disciples in the New Testament, as it declares "Now when they saw the boldness of Peter and John...they took knowledge of them, that they had been with Jesus"! Was this the same cowardly Peter so overcome with fear that he three times denied his Lord, twice to harmless women?

But here at Pentecost, the birthday of Jesus' church in Acts 2, Peter is boldly prosecuting the nation of Israel for the gravest sin ever committed, the "temporary" murder of their own Messiah, and this new-found boldness was the most radically conclusive evidence that he had been with Jesus!

What made the difference between the petrified and passively powerless pre-crucifixion Peter who denied Jesus, and this now boldly empowered Peter of Pentecost? God's answer is, the Peter of Pentecost had seen with his own eyes his resurrected Redeemer, and this fact alone caused him to lose all fear of mortal men and even death itself!

At Pentecost, as Jesus' followers proclaimed truth and exposed the Jewish leaders' murder of their own Messiah, their only prayer request to God was not sparing further opposition or harm, but "that with all boldness they may speak thy word" (Acts 4:29).

God obviously answered their courageous prayers, as the passage documents "And when they had prayed, the place was shaken…and they were all filled with the Holy Ghost, and they spake the Word of God with boldness" (Acts 4:31)!

Every truly saved pastor and layman today has figuratively visited the empty tomb and "seen the resurrected Christ" with spiritually opened eyes! So why are many of us still filled with fear of what sin-filled men inside or outside the church may do to us for protecting the spiritual purity of His bride, when Paul concluded "For me to live is Christ, and (even) to die is gain" (Philippians 1:21)?

Especially in more recent decades in America, it seems her churches have been saturated with vast infestations of merciful and encouraging pastors, ever ready to extend a loving and compassionate but strategically "position-preserving" response to carnal Christians. Obviously a Biblical balance of mercy and prophecy is essential to true Christ-like leadership in His church.

But when rendered in an unbalanced fashion, today's prophetic people-pleaser pastors tragically lack essential boldness and courage to address or rebuke sin when needed, likely evidencing that they have not really been "with Jesus" much if at all.

Most churches today readily prefer and embrace the soft and merciful exhorter who constantly encourages the people and makes them feel good about themselves in their spiritual condition, over the perceived "gloom and doom" prophets who dare to rock our comfortable boat or step on our spiritual toes, because our spiritual pride resists having our sins redemptively revealed and confronted.

Today's many passive people-pleaser pastors can be easily identified by their vast popularity and favor amongst a worldly brand of Christianity in many "user-friendly" churches today. They may lead large numbers in the church who on the surface appear to be numerically thriving and prosperous, but inwardly their unconfronted cancer of conformity to the world divinely renders their witness spiritually weak and powerless!

By contrast, not even our sin-less Lord Jesus was popular or liked by most sinners as evidenced by His very small number of followers, evidencing the tragic spiritual problem of popular but prophetically passive people-pleaser pastors today!

21

Jesus no doubt addresses this type of pastor and church in His great Sermon on the Mount - "Ye are the salt of the earth: but if the salt have lost his savor, wherewith shall it be salted? It is thenceforth good for nothing, but to be cast out and to be trodden under foot of men" (Matthew 5:13).

We all know salt is by its very nature a very effective flavor enhancement, but most "post-electricity Boomers and Busters" today may be too young to remember its valuable property as a powerful preservation agent!

Jesus paints a condemning picture of today's many popular people-pleaser pastors and churches who have apparently lost their impact as the God-ordained earthly sin-retarding agent, effectively becoming a worthless object of sinners' scorn – a sad but accurate description of a lost world's contempt and cynical attitude toward the widespread worldliness of today's church!

During my seminary days as staff member in a major church, I mournfully witnessed God's beloved bride "trodden under foot of men" in a most apocalyptically graphic way:

During the annual pagan ritual called "Mardi Gras" in New Orleans, instead of God's army surrounding His church to witness Christ's love and redemption or unrepentant judgment, many members routinely joined in the revelry, even allowing God's church building to actually help facilitate revelers' participation!

When this church's small remnant of faithful followers of Christ finished witnessing by distributing all the Bible tracts they had, they left the crowded parade route to return to their cars for departure. It was then that we witnessed the sordid sight of drunken revelers "relieving" themselves on the outside walls of the church and parking lot!

Now it must also be conceded that there are unbalanced prophets as well as unbalanced encouragers – prophecy gifted pastors perhaps lacking adequate mercy and compassion to balance their natural willingness to confront and rebuke sin.

But because of prophecy's primary Biblical motivation to proclaim truth and expose sin for the purpose of redemption, a true prophet even perceived to lack love and mercy is infinitely more vulnerable to rejection by most people even inside the church than the unbalanced encourager lacking courage to confront sin.

Accordingly, most people and churches will still love, accept and embrace an unbalanced encourager lacking boldness to confront sin, but usually resent and reject a prophet even if balanced with godly mercy and compassion, as Jesus "came unto his own, and His own received him not" (John 1:11).

This also spiritually explains why in the Old Testament, the reluctant weeping prophet Jeremiah endured such intense opposition, beatings and imprisonments for obediently proclaiming God's impending judgment on apostate Judah, and why the prophet Isaiah was, according to traditional speculation, martyred by being sawed in half inside a hollow log for obediently attacking the idolatry and social iniquities of their day!

These and many other faithful prophets were motivated solely by genuine love evidenced by their 23 concern for the spiritual destiny of people, willing to risk their own safety and life by condemning iniquity in effort to bring them to God. But instead of repenting and thanking these godly prophets, their own nation persecuted and often martyred them as a prophetic prelude to their future climactic rejection of Jesus the "Perfect Prophet"!

To perhaps more graphically illustrate the danger of today's passively weak people-pleaser pastors, consider a "hypothetical editing" of a tragic but true story that actually occurred in my hometown many years ago:

Imagine you are a motorist driving on a dark and foggy night across the world's longest bridge, which moments earlier had been struck by a passing barge wiping out a whole section. You casually continue, but suddenly without warning plunge to your death! You had no idea the section of bridge was missing and the night's poor visibility gave absolutely no warning that death was awaiting you!

The bridge officials you pass flashed no red lights or even sounded any urgent warning to save you, hesitating to confront you fearing they would offend you by "interfering with the direction of your own life". Thus, they merely give you a friendly and encouraging wave as you pass them by!

This is precisely what many pleasantly popular but spiritually unbalanced "people-pleaser" pastors today are doing in their churches, allowing members to plunge off sin's edge without ever boldly warning them, revealing why many "church members" today are falling prey to the enemy of our soul, Satan.

24    Though a stiff-necked and unrepentant society nev-

er desires negative warnings, today it is evident that America and especially her churches desperately need loving prophets braced with the courage to boldly sound the alarm of impending destruction, rather than the steady diet of today's prophetically passive people-pleaser pastors whose fear of man allows unrepentant iniquity to remain epidemic without warning!

Unfortunately, many pastors today will often do most anything to avoid confronting sin in the church, given the almost inevitable consequences they face in their lives and ministries for doing so. Our loving Heavenly Father compassionately understands this valid concern, particularly when there is a precious wife and family to provide for!

If this were our only source of concern, God simply reassures us "Seek ye first the kingdom of God...and all these things shall be added unto you" (Matthew 6:33). But temporary loss of our family's financial provision is not our only fear.

What many pastors usually fear more than temporary loss of income is what must be particularly grievous to God – prideful fear of damaging or losing our successful reputation and the resulting stigma and lingering doubts of many people, churches and even fellow-ministers toward us that usually accompany being cast out, even if for the cause of Christ.

Suddenly most churches, and even many denominational leaders and fellow-pastors may distance themselves, as doors of service opportunity seem to diminish now that they are stripped of their ministry status and labeled a controversial spiritual outcast by the "religious establishment".

Such was obviously the case for the sinless Lord Jesus, and even for George Whitefield of England, one of the world's greatest preachers and a leader of America's First Great Awakening from 1738 until his death in 1770.[2]

Whitefield boldly confronted sin within the church and preached the doctrine of the necessity of repentance and true heart salvation, which apparently threatened and offended many established clergy and churches in his native England. Thus they collectively rejected him and his message, virtually blackballing him from their pulpits.

This fact however did nothing to deter him from preaching to the masses wherever they would listen, then many times crossing the Atlantic to preach in America's colonies over the span of thirty years, usually at his own personal sacrifice having been spiritually and financially separated from support by his own home churches.

Though scorned and outcast by sinful men inside the church, God and history have duly affirmed George Whitefield as one of the world's greatest preachers and true prophets of God!

Unlike Whitefield however, for many prophetic people-pleaser pastors today the primary ministry goals are often identical to the typical secular world's vocational goals and aspirations –make friends (gain acceptance and popularity), influence people (establish our ministry status and reputation), and climb the ladder of success (attract bigger, more visible churches).

In addressing his own ministry the great apostle Paul posed a decisive question to reveal the pure motive for his life and work - "For do I now persuade men or God? or do I seek to please men? for if I yet pleased men, I should not be the servant of Christ" (Galatians 1:10).

Notice Paul used a particular adjective which describes many popular highly sought-after but spiritually weak pastors today – "men-pleasers" rather than servants of Christ, choosing to appease sinful men rather than God.

For this reason, pastors often tend to shy away from taking a spiritual stand in the church that would possibly offend habitual sinners, who's apathetic and chronically disobedient lifestyle subtly sabotages the witness of the church because we tragically compromise on our choice of who to please!

This is precisely why Joshua sternly challenged us to "Choose you this day whom ye will serve" (Joshua 24:15), since Jesus declared "No man can serve two masters" (Matthew 6:24)!

This seemingly harsh ultimatum of having to clearly choose between pleasing sinful men (even within the church) or a Holy God has always been the purest indicator of whether a pastor or preacher is a true man of God or simply a "puppet on a string" in the hands of fickle men. But many passively weak people-pleaser pastors attempt to conceal their puppet strings under the disguise of "mercy and compassion" and simply fail to confront or rebuke sin, thus ensuring the endearing acceptance and esteem of habitually disobedient and pacified sinners within the church.

When Jesus addressed the adulterous woman in John 8, He obviously had great mercy, compassion, and understanding for her, as not only did He not condemn her, but instead aimed His righteous indignation at her hypocritical accusers whom He knew were guilty of the same sin they were ready to stone her for! But unlike many passive people-pleaser pastors today, the righteous Lord Jesus did not allow His great mercy and compassion to accommodate or license her sin, as He redemptively instructed this woman "go and sin no more" (John 8:11).

James 2:13 tells us "mercy triumphs against judgment", and as under-shepherds for the Great Shepherd we obviously must administer His divine measure of mercy to sinful mankind, since "Blessed are the merciful, for they shall obtain mercy" (Matthew 5:7).

However, when mercy, love and compassion lack righteous discipline, they inevitably become passively licentiousness toleration of sin!

God's Word makes no eternal distinction between "big and little sins", as one "little" sin rendered Adam a sinner separated from God, though the earthly consequence of a boy taking a grape from the grocery store obviously pales compared to a man who commits murder! But most pastors and people still categorize sins based on earthly consequence!

But what types of serious "little sins" do prophetically passive people-pleaser pastors typically avoid confronting today?

Foremost to Jesus but typically ignored by us sinners are the sins of omission – failing to do what Jesus commands, often resulting in foolish use of that time for the sins of commission!

28

In Luke 19:10, Jesus revealed His ultimate purpose for coming to earth and establishing His church - "For the Son of man is come to seek and to save that which was lost". He then instructed His disciples "Follow Me, and I will make you fishers of men" (Matthew 4:19). So consider:

When is the last time you heard a pastor redemptively but boldly rebuke and chastise his church for apathetically failing to witness or even show up for evangelistic outreach?

Perhaps it is because many pastors themselves do not witness for Jesus since we are often so busy catering to the flock's seemingly endless needs - how sadly prophetic this must be to God.

We usually offer many reasons for this failure to witness, like "that is just not my gift!", "it conflicts with my busy work schedule" or "that is my child's ball game night", but these excuses usually reveal that Jesus' mission to save the lost is simply not our priority as "non-followers" of Jesus.

When is the last time you observed a pastor redemptively but boldly follow the Matthew 18 blueprint for church discipline by confronting an unrepentant member living in known sin and immorality, properly leading the church to formally vote for his removal from "membership in good standing", even if his resident address was 1600 Pennsylvania Avenue? How sadly prophetic this must be to God.

When is the last time you witnessed a pastor redemptively but boldly follow the Ezekiel 3:17 "Watchman" principle by confronting and warning wicked leaders in the church, government or society of the inevitably eternal consequences of their unrepentant wickedness, or even publicly commending a Godly leader for his righteous stand? How sadly prophetic this must be to God.

When is the last time you heard a pastor redemptively but boldly rebuke his congregation for finding every excuse in the book for being "MIA's" (missing-in-action) during worship or some ministry-related work requiring some sacrifice on their part, but heaping praises on them for being so faithful to attend church fellowship dinners ("meet and eats")? How sadly prophetic this must be to God.

When is the last time you heard a pastor redemptively but boldly confront his congregation for "lying" to God in church singing lip-service "Have Thine Own Way Lord" or "Worship, Work and Witness Till Jesus Comes", or for sitting in the pews like a "valley of dry bones" during congregational hymns to Him? How sadly prophetic this must be to God.

When is the last time you heard a pastor redemptively but boldly preach about the never-ending agony and torture of hell's flames and bottomless pit of outer darkness which tragically may await even many "respected church-goers" today based on Jesus' warning of Matthew 7:21 "Not everyone that saith unto me Lord, Lord, shall enter into the kingdom of heaven; but he that doeth the will of my Father"? How sadly prophetic this must be to God.

Many passively powerless people pleaser pastors in pulpits today have disdained the "dreadfully distasteful" duty to daringly declare that outwardly religious church members who give Jesus "lip service" on Sunday, with no desire or evidence of doing His will of evangelism and discipleship on Monday through Saturday, may actually be in danger of being the most shocked and horrified people on judgment day!

When is the last time you saw a pastor redemptively but boldly take an exclusive stand for traditional godly hymns, refusing to compromise God's church with today's more popular but often ungodly "contemporary" music, most of which tends to be nothing more than occasional mention of Jesus set to fleshly melodies of "rock and roll" – how sadly prophetic this must be to God.

For you see, Satan is also a very musically "piped" being (Ezekiel 28:13), and will cunningly use any available vessel to play melodies and lyrics that appease and call out to his demonic spirit and appeasing our flesh rather than the Spirit of God (I Samuel 16:23)!

Prophetically, it seems most pastors in America today are tragically unwilling to risk their positions by refusing to compromise Biblical principles in God's church amidst those who "hold the purse strings" financially sustaining them - how sadly prophetic this must be to God.

According to Jesus, this is the primary difference between a hireling and a shepherd – "the good shepherd giveth his life for the sheep, (but) the hireling fleeth, because he is an hireling, and careth not for the sheep" (John 10:11,13).

Because a true shepherd dearly loves the sheep, he is willing to confront any threat of harm to the flock, regardless of the potential danger to his own safety. But as a mere hired hand, the hireling has no vested interest in the sheep since he possesses no ownership, but merely cares for himself and would therefore never risk personal danger to pro-

31

tect the sheep.

Historically, perhaps the greatest challenge in the church is divinely distinguishing Satan's camouflaged wolves lurking within both ministry and laity today from His true sheep. Thus Jesus warns "Beware of false prophets, which come to you in sheep's clothing, but inwardly they are ravening wolves" (Matthew 7:15).

But in these perilous last days, because even many professing sheep spend precious little time with the Great Shepherd in His Word, their spiritual capability to discern the wolves in both pulpit and pew has largely faded.

But even if spiritually able to discern, many pastors are often mortally afraid to protect the sheep by confronting or publicly revealing the wolves for fear of offending! But "the preaching of the cross is to them that perish foolishness (offensive)" (I Corinthians 1:18).

My godly former pastor and spiritual mentor often declared, "I would rather lovingly and redemptively offend someone into heaven than liberally lull them into hell" - and he faithfully risked it! But tragically, it seems today's brand of passive people-pleaser pastors would often rather safely lull someone into hell than risk offending them into heaven - how sadly prophetic this must be to God.

Or how about this "taboo" subject – when is the last time you saw a pastor redemptively but boldly exhort a smoker or chewer to refrain from his sin in Jesus' Bride the church or feel free to exit His premises?

Husbands, imagine your wedding day standing at the altar beholding your beautifully adorned bride-to-be gracefully approaching you in her perfectly pristine white dress!

Then something utterly repulsive and shocking happens – one attendee inexplicably flicks cigarette ashes on her spotless dress and another spits tobacco juice on her beautiful vale. But her father strangely and passively ignores their deplorable behavior and does nothing to intervene on her behalf! How sadly prophetic this must be to God.

Perhaps the root explanation for much pastoral passivity toward sin is that we fearfully allow our virtuous desire to be "understanding and redemptive" toward people to translate into unbalanced toleration and licentious acceptance of sin.

Courageous under-shepherds love sinners with God's agape love, but hate and redemptively rebuke sin! Prophetically passive people-pleaser pastors render loving-kind mercy, but passively allow a haven for habitual sin in God's church. Obviously this is not true love at all, but passive permissiveness bringing great reproach to Christ and His church in the eyes of a now largely lost nation.

So for well over a half century in our Founders' beloved nation following an infamous national and world war, what other root problems have prophetically passive people-pleaser pastors largely helped initiate, and how have these root problems spiritually impacted America's churches and nation?

## Chapter Two

Spiritually Asleep "Sin-thetic" Sheep:

It is evident today that a primary consequence of many decades of prophetically passive people-pleaser pastors in America is a nation of churches often full of what God and our Founders may conceivably describe as "spiritually asleep sin-thetic sheep"!

In Matthew 13:24, Jesus revealed a prophetic parable (earthly example bearing eternal principle) about a good man who sowed good seed in his field, "but while men SLEPT, his enemy came and sowed tares among the wheat" resulting in devastating destruction!

In 2 Timothy 4:3-4, Paul further prophesied "For the time will come when they will not endure sound doctrine; but after their own lusts shall they heap to themselves teachers, having itching ears; and they shall turn away their ears from truth, and shall be turned unto fables".

Tragically, Jesus' divine parable seems to have profound application to post-World War II America, having valiantly and victoriously "fought the good fight" both militarily and physically, only to see her churches subtly lapse into a deep spiritual sleep, passively allowing the enemy (Satan) to deceive and endeavor to destroy the foundations which made her great!

America's Founders clearly understood Jesus' parable, declaring "Political slavery is ever preceded by sleep" (Founder John Dickinson),[3] as history itself reveals that spiritually for any nation, the only thing necessary for evil to triumph is for good men to do nothing!

Now lest subsequent generations self-righteously condemn America's so-called "greatest generation", we must compassionately comprehend just a couple of "minor" economic and political challenges faced in their lives:

After enduring a decade of epidemic economic Depression in the 1930's, the 1940's became their worst nightmare, as by the mid-1940's our brave surviving but war-ravaged soldiers finally emerged victorious in defeating a demonic dictator and his world-threatening allies, joyfully returning home understandably longing for peace, prosperity and a more normal life for their families than their generation had been destined for!

So they understandably began daily working hard to have and raise their "booming" families, merely endeavoring to provide the material "luxuries" most of them never had growing up – things like sufficient food, clothing and shelter perhaps even complete with indoor plumbing and utilities!

Often still physically, emotionally, psychologically and spiritually wounded by war's lingering effects on their personal lives and vocation, most came home to their families on weekends for the first time able to enjoy some fruits of their labor, as Saturday was often their day to enjoy ballgames or other recreational escapes with their families!

Sundays often were the day when families hopefully went to church to likely hear pastors gently and compassionately massaging ears with an initially-needed diet of encouraging optimistic messages of comfort. Then they went home preparing to restart the cycle of another week, as life was finally starting to seem good for many surely deserving military heroes!

Slowly one by one, many "good men" began to quietly leave "politics" in favor of the more economically rewarding and time availing private sector, creating a grave spiritual "vacuum" in many public arenas, especially government!

Elementary science class correctly teaches us that a "scientific vacuum" is artificially created when all substances including air molecules are forced out of an object, leaving a total void of any air or substance inside. Interestingly enough, it is not natural for this vacuum to remain, as this "void" will naturally seek to draw back into itself whatever exists on the outside, whether good or bad!

This is slowly and subtly what happened in America's churches regarding public arenas like government, as good men tragically began to spiritually fall asleep. Though the enemy has always tried and often succeeds in many undiscerning churches, America's post-war spiritually asleep churches saw Satan begin to epidemically infest His church with many "tares among the wheat", subsequently opening the flood gates of infestation in government and other public arenas with many wicked and corrupt "politicians" (see "REDISCOVERING America's Republic").

The national consequences of this prophetic cross-generational spiritual slumber and turning from God's true doctrine are documented in the next two root problem sections! But the reason we will spend more time on "Sin-thetic" sheep instead of on "Spiritually Asleep" sheep is because it was sin that caused His churches to spiritually fall asleep in the first place, as the only hope for America is for God's churches and true sheep to repent and spiritually wake up (2 Chronicles 7:14)!

Will America's churches repent and wake up? - only God truly knows that answer. When evil struck a devastating blow directly upon our personal circle of concern on an infamous day in 1941, America woke up! But apparently another infamous day in 2001 only slightly and temporarily nudged us!

But what is meant by the seemingly satirical description "sin-thetic" sheep? Before explaining, we should first identify the Biblical evidence of true sheep according to Jesus! Jesus reveals at least five types of "creatures" in His church – "submissive sheep" (John 10:27), "straying sheep" ("sin-thetic" - John 10:16), "goats" (aggressive instinct and impulse - Matthew 25:32), "camouflaged wolves" (disguised as sheep - Matthew 7:15), and "obvious wolves" (no attempt to disguise - John 10:12).

By nature, submissive sheep of the pasture never endeavor to purposefully harm the flock but also innately lack defense against predators, which reveals why their very survival depends on heeding the shepherd's voice!

In John 10:27, Jesus reveals the conclusive evidence of His submissive sheep - "My sheep hear My voice, and I know them, and they follow Me". Submissive sheep listen for the shepherd's voice and obediently follow Him. Wolves and goats cannot, for it is not their nature to do so, but only follow their own fleshly instincts at the expense of the sheep.

This is God's primary distinction between submissive sheep and straying "sin-thetic" sheep.

According to Jesus, as His submissive sheep faithfully follow the Great Shepherd, an amazing transformation occurs, as He commanded Peter "Follow me, and I will make you fishers of men" (Matthew 4:19). As submissive sheep closely follow Jesus through His Word, they will inevitably become so filled with His love for lost sinners that they will be compelled to endeavor to draw others into God's kingdom!

According to Webster's Dictionary, the word "synthetic" means "produced artificially rather than of natural origin". Often it is very difficult or impossible for our naked eye to distinguish between something genuine and synthetic, as only properly trained personnel can usually accurately distinguish! For example, the U.S. Currency Mint's personnel are so routinely and thoroughly exposed to real dollar bills that when a counterfeit is secretly passed through their fingers, they can usually detect it immediately!

Thankfully in God's church, it is not our job to ultimately discern an individual's true identity as a wolf, goat or sheep (submissive or sin-thetic), for the Righteous Judge has the last word on that!

But as objective fruit inspectors, Jesus instructs us to discern what kind of tree it is by objectively observing the fruit it produces, "Wherefore by their fruits ye shall know them" (Matthew 7:20).

In my beloved denomination today, statistics on annual conversions now indicate that it takes over thirty-five "sheep" a whole year to produce one "born again" (John 3:3) sheep for Christ. Given this reproachful rate of reproductive growth, even a normal rate of annual mortal attrition would soon put these sheep on the "endangered species" list!

Based on this evidence, it would seem apparent that either these sheep's spiritual reproductive systems are grossly malfunctioned by sin or many of these "sin-thetic straying sheep" may actually be spiritually lost!

Many churches today are often filled with obvious wolves, camouflaged wolves and ungodly goats. But even amongst the sheep, Jesus left the ninety-nine to seek after one lost or straying sheep (Matthew 18:12), indicating the possibility of perhaps being a true sheep, but straying from the shepherd via sin. This surely describes even truly saved church members at isolated times in our lives, as opposed to the habitual pattern of the lost!

Whether sin-thetic sheep are truly saved or not only they and God ultimately know for sure. But according to Jesus, submissive sheep follow the Great Shepherd and reproduce more sheep, and He promised we can know them by their harvest of more sheep!

But it is sadly possible and perhaps even likely that many "professing sheep" in the church will never produce even one new sheep for Christ and are perhaps incapable of doing so because they are actually spiritually lost!

According to Christ, this type of sin-thetic sheep does not follow Him, but strays from the shepherd and their spiritual fishing nets are sadly unused. They might even be nice, loving and decent people within the church. But when it comes to witnessing for Jesus outside the church, they flee from the shepherd and are nowhere to be found – they go their own way and reproduce no new sheep.

Typically however, it is these same lost or straying sheep who often hold leadership positions of great influence on decisions affecting the church's witness and effectiveness in fulfilling Jesus' Great Commission to evangelize and disciple, since being in control of their own direction and influencing others accordingly is of utmost importance to sin-thetic sheep – but submissive sheep faithfully endeavor to follow truth!

The truth is, any "church" who fails to follow Jesus as fishers of men in striving to witness Christ's salvation to the lost is really not a church at all according to Jesus, regardless of what the building sign may claim, but has slowly degenerated over many years into a man-made club whose practiced pattern of spiritual hibernation in their weekly religious ritual has slowly and subtly over many years replaced the mission of Christ!

This tragic scenario sadly describes many so-called churches today, likely started long ago by a small but spiritually zealous core group of evangelistic charter members committed to soul-winning, but slowly over the

41

generations through pride, apathy or stubbornness subtly left their first love, becoming content to play church in their comfortable clubhouse.

Thus Revelation 3:20 says, "Behold, I stand at the door and knock, if any man hear My voice and open the door, I will come in to him and will sup (fellowship) with him and he with Me"! This prophetically describes a vast majority of churches in America today, as Jesus stands outside gently knocking at the door seeking entrance into His own church, but her occupants refuse to let Him in!

So before America will ever see God restored in her government and other public arenas, America's churches must first repent and wake up to hear His knock, renouncing our pride to humbly allow God back into His own church!

Thus it is ironic that as with the Pharisees toward Jesus, that a godly pastor's primary source of opposition and persecution today does not usually come from the lost world outside the church, but from religious leaders within (deacons, committee chairmen, etc) whose spiritual apathy and fleshly-minded hearts preclude them from following Christ as fishers of men.

Perhaps nowhere is this lack of follow-ship more evident than in how we often carry out church government.

My particular beloved denomination's local churches deeply cherish our "autonomous congregational government", the local church's supposed independence to oversee their own decisions and actions free of any denominational interference or accountability.

As professing "People of the Book" scripturally attesting to the "Priesthood of the Believer" (a believer's direct access to God through Christ the only mediator - 2 Timothy 3:5-6), my beloved denomination's local churches duly affirm the Bible as our only source of authority for faith and practice, but often sadly exert their "autonomy" in the practice of their faith according to personal interpretation of scripture!

However, 2 Peter 1:20 declares "no prophecy of the scripture is of any PRIVATE interpretation - for prophecy came not in old time by the will of man, but holy men of God spake as they were moved by the Holy Ghost"!

Thus the Bible came from God and not from sinful man, and is therefore not subject to our own personal "interpretations", no matter how sincere or well-intended they may be since God's is the only one that ultimately and authoritatively matters!

However, God's authoritative meaning may indeed have multiple varied applications to each personal life and experiences - or as a loving but boldly prophetic pastor correctly used to say about the Bible, "There is only one divine interpretation, but many possible earthly applications"!

But God knew He obviously could not trust the deeply flawed understandings, perspectives and meanings that sinful men would tend to impose upon scripture in order to accommodate our own carnal desires.

Yet this is usually what many local churches do under total autonomy, attaching and practicing their own personal interpretation of scripture with no earthly denominational accountability. The almost inevitable result of

43

local church autonomy with no earthly accountability is often epidemic doctrinal error or perverted practice of doctrine.

This explains the existence of so many doctrinally diverse Protestant denominations during more than four centuries since Martin Luther's watershed "Ninety-five Theses" gave birth to the Protestant Reformation!

Hence, many non-Protestants (especially Roman Catholics) quite understandably may perceive this seeming "doctrinal diversity" and lack of uniformity among many different Protestant faiths as seeming confirmation and evidence of doctrinal deviance from "the faith"!

Scripturally, their perception likely bears some validity since "God is not the author of confusion, but of peace" (I Corinthians 14:33).

But it must also be pointed out that Luther's landmark doctrine of "salvation through faith alone apart from works" represented the very first Evangelical doctrinal effort based on sole authority of Scripture after more than twelve centuries under Roman authority dating back to the early fourth century when Christianity, which for three centuries had been severely persecuted and martyred by the Romans, became diluted by this powerful political empire as its "official religion" under Emperor Constantine.[4]

Since the Bible is God's divine Word, Luther's ninety-five theses as profoundly insightful as they were, were not an "all-inclusive finished work" but were merely Luther's landmark effort on the doctrine of salvation by faith alone as a solid theological foundation upon which further doctrine consistent with "all scripture" (2 Timothy 3:16) could be divinely developed under the tutelage of the Holy

Spirit across generations, as even Jesus Himself declared "My doctrine is not mine, but His that sent me" (John 7:16).

However, the truth remains that autonomy with no measure of earthly spiritual or denominational accountability usually leads to scriptural deviation, erroneous doctrine or practice, and gross toleration of Biblical violations, a problem which if not addressed will likely threaten at least my particular denomination's very survival.

But sin-thetic sheep usually want the freedoms and blessings of the Great Shepherd, but characteristically refuse to follow Him by insisting on doing what is "right in (their) own eyes" (Proverbs 21:2).

Being from the predominantly Catholic city of New Orleans, Louisiana, I've personally observed that autonomy with no earthly accountability is understandably a primary stumbling block against Protestant Evangelical Christianity for most Catholics and even many others, as their concern bears some Biblical validity and merit.

Contrastingly however, it is mandatory for Catholics to submit to accountability toward denomination's hierarchy, traditions and control, lacking freedom or encouragement to read and discern God's truth of the Bible themselves.

As with our nation's erroneously perceived form of government (see Myth of Demonic "Democracy"), in many mainline Protestant churches church government is usually perceived and practiced as a democracy rather than the theocracy God created His church to be. In fact, some church constitutions describe their church government using various words to this effect, "This church is a democra-

45

cy, whose authority is vested in the majority of her members"! But by definition in a theocracy, God rules over His church as Jesus declared "All power (authority) is given unto Me in heaven and in earth" (Matthew 28:18). Every submissive sheep in His theocratic church will endeavor to submit to the will of Christ as revealed through His Word or she is not His submissive sheep!

The greatest example of this sacrificial submission was evidenced before His crucifixion, as Jesus prayed to His Father "not My will, but Thine be done" (Luke 22:42). But dying to our will is something "straying sin-thetic sheep" will usually not do. They usually do whatever the majority says, even if it violates what God says!

This is why the "democratic congregational government" practiced in many churches today is simply not scriptural, since it is not "congregations or the majority" who are to govern God's church, but Christ Himself by His Word through His submissive sheep!

In many churches today, many sin-thetic sheep may "verbally" concede the right of Christ to rule His church, but in "practice" blatantly usurp the authority of His Word, insisting on "their opinion" no matter what God says.

Since in practice even Christ's ultimate authority is frequently challenged and violated, it is no wonder why many pastors are essentially allowed little or no authority to lead His church, even if he is personally faithful in endeavoring to follow and lead His sheep to follow Christ and His Word!

In fact, the issue of "pastoral authority" is probably the most sensitive and controversial subject among many sin-thetic sheep in churches today, a somewhat understandable church reaction due to the growing moral and doctrinal failures of many pastors in our day.

Today even submissive sheep quite understandably must be spiritually discerning before investing their trust in a leader, since trust must be earned by his walk with God and obeying His Word.

But once a congregation bestows their vote of trust by calling a pastor based on observed spiritual integrity and faithfulness to God's Word, unless subsequent moral or doctrinal failure is clearly evidenced, submissive sheep are to willingly follow his scriptural leadership according to God's admonition, "Obey them that have the rule over you and submit yourselves, for they watch for your souls, as they that must give account, that they may do it with joy and not with grief, for that is unprofitable for you" (Hebrews 13:17).

Not so with sin-thetic sheep and wolves, who must use their power, position, wealth, family status and reputation to impose their own authority and will over a godly pastor and even Christ! These "sheep" simply will not be led, but stray from the Great Shepherd and His faithful under-shepherd in order to appease their own spiritual pride and status through their obsessive need to control or influence others.

People-pleaser pastors in this type of church usually cower to pressure and passively "stay in line" in order to preserve their position, reputation and career. They convince themselves that if they just "love and encourage" the people, they will eventually "come around"! But as actual shepherds of the pasture know, habitual straying sheep must usually be isolated by abandonment or expulsion in order to protect the flock from their destructive influence.

However, if the number of sin-thetic sheep, goats and wolves exceeds the number of submissive sheep in many of today's churches, it will be the pastor who's promptly "terminated", symbolic of their treatment of Christ!

The explanation usually given for this action by these sin-thetic sheep and wolves is "things just didn't work out", "he just couldn't fit in" or "we just did not like him"! Then they systematically form another search committee to find another "sacrificial lamb".

But Jesus declares "Blessed are ye when men shall hate you, and when they shall separate you from their company, and shall reproach you, and cast out your name as evil for the Son of man's sake – Rejoice ye in that day, for your reward is great in heaven, for in the like manner did their fathers unto the prophets" (Luke 6:22-23).

But a godly pastor must always remember that the wolves, goats and sin-thetic straying sheep are not his true enemies, but Satan himself who merely works through his pawns "to steal, to kill and to destroy" (John 10:10).

Since the church is the bride of Christ, and since Christ assigns responsibility to His faithful under-shepherds to protect and lead His bride, it is no mystery why godly pastors and leaders have always been Satan's primary target of attack on earth, for he knows if he can sabotage the under-shepherd, he can more easily ravage the flock.

In most of America's churches today, it is the lack of church discipline which plagues the body of Christ via many cowardly passive pastors afraid to confront sin and their sin-thetic sheep who want to have it both ways, living like the world Monday through Saturday but still assimilating spiritual status via church membership and professed heavenly destiny.

Unrepentant sins that once would have resulted in loss of church membership are now seemingly embraced as common-place in the name of toleration and cultural acceptance. What types of sins are we talking about?

Well consider, once upon a time in America's churches, if an unrepentant member had chronically unjustified absences and failure to spiritually support his church, that member was Biblically liable to be brought before the church and possibly removed from the membership roll. Today, such people are usually merely referred to as "inactive members"!

Once upon a time, if a member got divorced even for Biblically allowable reasons ("fornication" Matthew 19:9 or "unbelieving spouse departs" I Corinthians 7:15), and subsequently violated scripture by remarrying another (I Corinthians 7:11), that member was Biblically an "adulterer" (Matthew 19:9) and if unrepentant, a candidate for dismissal.

But today, sin-thetic sheep often refer to them as "deacons or committee chairmen", elevating them as a model of Christian family and leadership in the church!

Once upon a time, if a thrice confronted but unrepentant member was found in possession of or given over to such vices as alcohol, tobacco, cigarettes, drugs, pornography, gambling or the like, he was Biblically a "heathen and a publican" (Matthew 18:17) and was removed from membership. Today, sin-thetic sheep usually call them "good ole boys" and crown them as church ushers.

Once upon a time, if an unrepentant male member had long hair, he was redemptively confronted with I Corinthians 11:14 "Doth not even nature itself teach you that if a man have long hair, it is a shame unto him?", and admonished to comply with the Biblical standard or forfeit his leadership position. Today, sin-thetic sheep often refer to these men as "contemporary Christian singers"!

Once upon a time, if an unrepentant member was observed even entering a movie containing profane language or indecency, that member was disciplined and ultimately even brought before the church to be disbanded from membership. Today, sin-thetic sheep often pack up the church van and call this "church movie night out"!

Once upon a time, if an unrepentant female member came to church dressed provocatively or immodestly, she was politely but firmly welcomed to return in modest apparel or simply stay home. Today, sin-thetic sheep often call this "contemporary fashion" and invite them into the choir!

And once upon a time, if a member was guilty of infidelity against his or her spouse, that member was Biblically an "adulterer" and if he remained unrepentant after being confronted by the pastor and another witness or two, was also brought before the church to be counted a "heathen and a publican" (Matthew 18:17).

For much of the 1990's, sin-thetic sheep in one particular Arkansas church passively retained and merely addressed this member as "Mister President"!

Because we have allowed our own "majority opinions", worldly television, movies, books, newspapers, magazines, media and internet to virtually supplant the Bible as our basis of thinking and practice, hundreds of local churches in America are tragically dying each year. But Christ's true church will obviously reign ultimately victorious over Satan and death, as "they overcame him by the Blood of the Lamb and by the Word of their testimony" (Revelation 12:11).

But according to Jesus, unregenerate wolves and goats in the church will one day anguish in eternity, as will even many unregenerate pastors, church leaders and sin-thetic straying "sheep" on Judgment Day as Jesus regretfully professes to them "I never knew you: depart from Me, ye that work iniquity" (Matthew 7:23).

Many "sin-thetic sheep" in churches today are deceived to believe it does not really matter whether we faithfully "live" for Christ and do what He says, since nobody does everything He says anyway, as long as we verbally profess salvation, get dunked in a baptistry and maybe show up for church occasionally.

But the Bible says "faith without works is dead" (James 2:20), as Jesus declares the evidence of phony faith is it verbally espouses God, but does not do His will (Matthew 7:21).

This is the reason the Watchman's warning in Ezekiel 3:17-19 is so critical not only to lost people but to professing Christians as well, because according to Matthew 7:13, a vast majority of the earth's population are going to reap the devil's eternal destruction in their unrepentance, and nothing will change this due to the hardness of their hearts.

But if God's people do not want hands stained with their blood, we must heed God's mission to warn and try to win them to Christ!

So as offensive as it may seem, here is one version of God's redemptively loving but righteous warning to unrepentant lost sinners inside and outside the church – "I so love you and want to redeem you – wisely redeem the time and turn, or sadly burn"!

Please ask Jesus to forgive your sins and save you through His shed blood into the Lamb's Book of Life while there's still time! Otherwise, the Bible declares "whosoever was not found written in the book of life was cast into the lake of fire" (Revelation 20:15).

And here is God's warning to any saved but straying sheep in the church who have strayed from the shepherd – "Repent, or soon be ushered to heaven", because Romans 8:13 warns carnal Christians "If ye live after the flesh ye shall die"!

That is, if a truly saved person backslides and continues to follow after his own sinful impulses, one day God will abruptly declare "You've brought enough reproach to My name" and will allow him to be physically removed from this life in order to avoid further reproach to His name!

So what primary effects have prophetically passive people-pleaser pastors and spiritually asleep sin-thetic sheep in America's churches ultimately had upon the nation at large? The answer is profoundly tragic, as Satan was passively allowed to sow two priority Myths of Demonic Deception upon a now largely Bible and Constitution illiterate and easily deceived society, the results of which continue to spiritually plague and threaten to destroy America today!

## Chapter Three

Myth of Demonic "Democracy":

Today in America, if the media took a public "opinion poll" asking our beloved nation: "What form of government is America?" – what do you think the "majority" in America would say?

Based on responses we've received even in many of America's churches today, you would likely find that most citizens of today's strategically-deprived generations on America's officially-documented history instinctively reply "America is a democracy"!

Even one former Republican Governor of Louisiana, when posed with this very unexpected question by an insightful inquirer, revealed his "politically-correct" but "double-minded" lack of knowledge by answering, "We are a democratic Republic"!

If you further asked Americans today, "Why do you believe this"? – most would likely refer to Abraham Lincoln's historically profound but not official national document, the Gettysburg Address: "that this nation, under God, shall have a new birth of freedom – and that government of the people, by the people, for the people, shall not perish from the earth"!

But consider that the Gettysburg Address is the only document that can even remotely be "assumed" to refer to democracy, as not one official founding document (Preamble, Constitution, Declaration of Independence, Bill of Rights, etcetera) ever mentions the words "democracy or democratic"! An important side note - proponents of this demonic myth of "democracy" now challenge President Dwight Eisenhower's insertion of "under God" in our Pledge of Allegiance in 1954, claiming lack of constitutional or primary source document basis of support!

Apparently proponents of "democracy" conveniently oppose America's "Great Emancipator" of African-American slavery's profound Gettysburg Address!

But as we will further see ("REDISCOVERING America's Republic"), according to our Founders the primary difference between a mere democracy and our form of government is their source of authority!

According to Webster's dictionary, a democracy's source of authority is "simple majority rule", a form of government where each citizen enjoys equal voting privilege to determine election outcome, without submission to divine authority or absolute right and wrong in personal accountability for his vote, since a sin-flawed subjective majority is its only earthly source of authority!

Thus hypothetically in a practicing democracy, if a referendum was offered to the voters and a fifty-one percent majority voted that murder should no longer be considered a crime, then murder would be legalized in America's present practicing democracy – just ask "Roe versus Wade"!

Historically, mankind's darkest hour and most wicked example of what a democracy (or "mob-rule" per Founders) can do is found in Matthew 27:17, as Roman governor Pontius Pilate attempted to abdicate his responsibility by catering to the angry mob when he asked, "Whom will ye that I release unto you, Barabbas or Jesus, which is called Christ"?

Matthew 27:22 prophetically reveals that the vast majority in this "demonic democracy" cast their ballots to crucify God's perfect sin-less Holy Son!

Now obviously the supremely sovereign Biblical God triumphed even over this devilish democracy by allowing it to be the very means of fulfilling His divine plan to offer His Son as the sacrificial lamb to shed His sin-less blood for the sin of mankind!

However, nations or individuals must never tempt God by assuming His sovereignty will divinely compensate for the fickle impulses and actions of a sin-flawed subjective majority, as Paul warned "Be not deceived; God is not mocked: for whatsoever a man soweth, that shall he also reap" (Galatians 6:7).

Hence in nations (as well as in churches), a democracy is potentially as dangerous as a dictatorship, since the only thing Satan has to do to accomplish his demonic plan is to influence the mind of one wicked ruler or the minds of a sin-flawed subjective majority!

So why do I dare label democracy as "demonic"? Well consider just a few of the many profound warnings against democracy from America's Founders:

"A simple democracy is the devil's own government" –
Founder Benjamin Rush.[5]

Founder Fisher Ames wisely warned "A democracy is
a volcano which conceals the fiery materials of its own destruction - these will produce an eruption and carry desola-
tion in their way – the known propensity of a democracy is to
licentiousness, which the ambitious call and ignorant believe
to be liberty"![6]

Founder John Adams further admonished "Remem-
ber, a democracy never lasts long; it soon wastes, exhausts and
murders itself – there never was a democracy yet that did not
commit suicide"![7]

Founder-President Thomas Jefferson declared "A democracy is nothing more than mob rule, where fifty-one percent of the people may take away the rights of the other for-
ty-nine percent"![8]

And Founder Benjamin Franklin prophetically
warned "When the people find that they can vote themselves
money, that will herald the end of the Republic"![9]

America's Founders wisely understood and heeded
God's warnings against trusting a majority of sin-flawed people, since "The heart is deceitful above all things, and desperately wicked: who can know it"? (Jeremiah 17:9) - "For the
love of money is the root of all evil, which while some coveted after…have erred from the faith and pierced themselves…
with many sorrows" (I Timothy 6:10)!

Yet many wicked politicians and citizens, and even some misguided American "conservatives" today still insist we are a democracy, primarily due to the fact that after 1947 much of our Founders' documentation of our nation's true history began slowly disappearing from the history books of America's public schools, yielding generations strategically deceived to believe America is a "pluralistic secular democracy"!

They insist that our Founders were a group of "pluralistic secularists" dedicated to a government in which all authority and power is placed in the hands of a majority of sin-flawed people where all religions, whether Biblically-based or not are welcomed in America's "majority-ruled democracy" (see "REDISCOVERING America's Republic")!

So why is exposing this myth of demonic democracy so important to God, our Founders and America's survival as a nation? What would America's faithful though surely not perfect Founders, who sacrificed their "lives, fortunes and sacred honor" (Declaration of Independence) to birth our beloved nation, think or say if they could see our moral and spiritual degeneration in just the past half-century or more?

At the very heart of this demonic myth is the disclaimer of the existence of any divinely objective moral absolutes of basic right and wrong upon which all nations can choose to honor and be blessed or violate and be cursed, rebelliously choosing to reject the existence or right of any sovereign authority over them in order to do the will of the sin-flawed majority!

Our Founders understood the root problem of this philosophy as found in Proverbs 14:12 "There is a way which seemeth right unto a man, but the end thereof are the ways of death", and Proverbs 21:2 "Every way of a man is right in his own eyes: but the Lord pondereth the hearts"!

In recent decades, America and even many churches have actually contributed to the peril of these last days by practicing as a democracy, apathetically living as though we no longer need God in nation, passively allowing prayer, the Bible and Ten Commandments removed from schools, attacks on the sanctity of human life via the murder of unborn children and the sanctity of God-ordained marriage via sanction of sodomy!

As a result, generations of school children deprived the right to see "Thou shalt not kill" (Exodus 20:13) are now the very ones now epidemically murdering in our schools and public places. America has now "legally" murdered over fifty million unborn children since 1973 with a national budget bombarded by escalating economic costs of abortion, and many lives tragically self-destructing in sodomy, reaping the sky-rocketing national health price tag of "Acquired Immune Deficiency Sin-drome"!

And in 2001, America's homeland received her worst political attack in exactly sixty years, as God redemptively but righteously attempts to humble an arrogantly puffed up nation and leaders to our knees!

America's wise Founders understood that wicked rulers are merely God's mournful judgment against nations' wicked living – "When the righteous are in authority the people rejoice; but when the wicked beareth rule the people mourn" Proverbs 29:2!

That is why Founder and "Father of Bill of Rights" George Mason prophetically declared, "As nations cannot be rewarded or punished in the next world, so they must be in this; by an inevitable chain of causes and effects, Providence (God) punishes national sins by national calamities",[10] evidencing our Founders' collective understanding on the earthly restriction of national blessing or cursing!

In his final Farewell Address, Founder-President and "Father of Nation" George Washington declared "Of all the dispositions and habits which lead to political prosperity, religion and morality are indispensable supports; in vain would that man claim the tribute of patriotism who should labor to subvert these great pillars"![11]

According to the "Father of our Nation", any citizen or public leader regardless of political party affiliation, whose agenda is to "subvert these great pillars" (Bible-based religion and morality) not only cannot claim patriotism, but has actually evidenced himself a traitor to America by subverting the very foundations of her survival and blessing!

The question God and our beloved Founders must be prophetically asking us today is, "Will America REPENT and REJOICE again by returning to righteousness, or will we continue mourning over our own wickedness to the prophetic point of no return"?

Prophetically, as America began to practice as a demonic democracy by trusting in mere "majority rule", it tragically led to yet another primary plague of demonic deception upon our nation!

## Chapter Four

Myth of "Separation of Church and State":

If a second public opinion poll posed the question to America, "Do you believe in Separation of Church and State, and if so WHY"? – today many even across political party lines may likely reply "Yes, because it is in the First Amendment"!

Yet this controversial phrase is not found in the First Amendment, Constitution or any other official founding document, as the First Amendment simply states:

"Congress shall make NO law respecting AN establishment of religion, or prohibiting the FREE exercise thereof…"!

According to U.S. Congressional Records dated June 7 to September 25, 1789, our Founders' two-fold First Amendment Intent was simply to: 1) prohibit government sanction of one denomination as the "national religion", but also to 2) ensure the inclusion and influence of God's Biblical principles in government![12]

Based on this official documentation, our Founders' purpose for their First Amendment was to keep government from establishing an official national church or denomination of Christianity as faced in England, but ensure inclusion and influence of Biblical principles' in America's public arenas including government!

America's Founders officially documented this desire to ensure the spiritual influence of God's principles in government and elections, but to keep government from interposing upon God's churches! To put it plainly, their First Amendment separated government from churches, not church influence and God's principles from government!

But today's proponents of demonic democracy impose their own meaning to this mythical phrase, claiming the Founders' wanted to separate God's churches from any influence upon government, while not as enthusiastically keeping government from interfering with churches (see following regarding IRS Code "501c3")!

So WHERE did this mythical phrase originate, and HOW have so many been deceived into thinking it was part of our Constitution?

On October 7, 1801, the Danbury Association of American Baptists in Danbury, Connecticut mailed a letter to newly elected President Thomas Jefferson, expressing their deep concern over a circulating rumor that a particular denomination was about to be established as the "national religion"![13]

On January 1, 1802, Jefferson personally and privately replied reassuring that "The First Amendment has erected a wall of separation between Church (which Jefferson defined as a federally established denomination) and State"![14] This private personal letter from Jefferson went appropriately unnoticed for almost one hundred and fifty years!

Then in the 1947 case of "Everson versus Board of Education", the court quoted only eight words of Jefferson's letter – "A wall of separation between Church and State", but added "that wall must be kept high and impregnable".[15] After 1947, the Supreme Court falsely concluded "This is what the Founding Fathers wanted - Separation of Church and State"!

But in a 1958 case called "Baer versus Kolmorgen", a dissenting judge rightly and profoundly warned "Continuing talk about Separation of Church and State would make people think it was part of the Constitution"![16] Indeed, William James (the so-called "Father of Modern Psychology") claimed "There is nothing so absurd but that if you repeat it often enough, people will believe it"![17]

Particularly since 1947, America has seen many destructive consequences of these two Myths of Demonic Deception on a now often Bible and Constitution illiterate and easily deceived society, as Proverbs 14:34 warns "Righteousness exalteth a nation, but sin is a reproach to any people" (even America)!

God and America's Founders would likely grievously remind us today that if some well intended church members had not given credence to a mere rumor, this mythical phrase and today's attached false meaning would likely never have come into existence to aid in the satanic separation of God from government!

Consider just a few of the mortal spiritual attacks on America:

One of Satan's early spiritual attacks was Charles Darwin's 1859 book "On the Origin of Species", which first introduced his infamous theory of "evolution".[18] But as damaging to America and our Biblical foundation of Creation as it was even to this very day, it was demonic democracy's slow but subtle replacement of the Bible with "majority rule" that rendered America increasingly vulnerable to Darwin's non-Biblical theory!

In 1954, a cunning tactic by Texas politician Lyndon Johnson, who was no ally to churches for their refusal to politically support him took assault! Under the guise of further ensuring their tax-exempt status, he added churches to the Internal Revenue Service's Code "501c3", but was actually intended to silence the voice of churches by prohibiting public endorsement of candidates, or lose their tax-exempt status![19]

This unprecedented new law clearly violated the First Amendment's "Congress shall make NO law... prohibiting the FREE exercise thereof" clause by imposing a law clearly attempting to limit the free exercise of religion and churches!

The truth is, churches in America have always been protected from taxation and government interference by Founders' First Amendment, which officially and legally placed churches outside of government jurisdiction, though as individual citizens her members surely remain subject to the laws of the land like all citizens!

So where did our Founders' get such a profound idea as "church tax-exempt status" (see "REDISCOVERING America's Republic")? And since 1954, how many churches in America have lost their First Amendment-guaranteed tax-exempt status for "violating" Code 501c3 by publicly endorsing candidates? The official answer to this crucial question is none![20]

So why do so many churches today live in fear of this "Code" or even bother seeking the IRS' permission for a tax-exemption already protected by First Amendment? It likely occurs out of: 1) innocent ignorance ("We did not know any better"), 2) bandwagon logic ("Everyone else is doing it") and 3) unsound professional advice of many attorneys and Certified Public Accountants!

As a result, for over a half century America's churches have largely remained passively silent from exercising their Founder-bestowed right to help influence public policy in government, frozen in fear by the "lame" threat of losing their coveted tax-exempt status.

In 1962, the turning point case of "Engel versus Vitale" effectively attempted to remove prayer, the Bible and postings of Ten Commandments from America's public schools, claiming violation of the mythical phrase "Separation of Church and State".[21]

The "controversy" in this case was a so-called "Unconstitutional Prayer", a non-denominational voluntary school prayer written by the New Hyde Park, New York state board of regents, which a few parents apparently claimed contradicted their religious beliefs! This twenty-two word non-sectarian voluntary prayer simply read:

"Almighty God, we acknowledge our dependence on Thee, and we beg Thy blessings upon us, our parents, our teachers and our country, Amen"!

This generic prayer made only one reference to God, the same as our Pledge of Allegiance and three less than our Declaration of Independence, and evidenced no embracement of any distinct doctrinal beliefs of a particular denomination!

The court reported that only three percent of America did not believe in God, evidencing that this so-called "Unconstitutional Prayer" was consistent with the beliefs of ninety-seven percent of our nation, marking the first time even in America that three percent had become a "majority"!

Then in 1963 one woman (Madalyn O'Hair), a primary instigator behind this and other cases founded the group "American Atheists",[22] evidencing her personal hatred for God, America's faithful Founders and our form of government!

Ten years later in 1973, the case of "Roe versus Wade" rendered a severe blow to the sanctity of human life by "legalizing" the murder of innocent unborn babies in America,[23] as even the Commandment "Thou shalt not kill" was no longer allowed as a "deterant" since the Bible itself was no longer the source of authority in their now practicing democracy!

But proponents of the myths of demonic "democracy" and "separation of church and state" are obviously not finished, as Satan's efforts have continued for decades to mortally wound the sanctity of the God-ordained family and attempting sanction of today's politically-correct "same-sex" but Bible-declared sodomite "marriage", which according to Scripture is not marriage!

These tragic consequences and many others in our unrepentance have happened to America because she relatively recently cast aside her divine source of authority to trust in mere "majority rule"!

Statistics in America since 1963 reveal the following:

- Divorce up over 117 %,
- Single-parent households up over 140 %,
- Sexually Transmitted Diseases (STD's) up over 226%,
- Premarital Sex up over 271%,
- Unmarried couples (Bible calls "fornication") up over 536%,
- Unwed Pregnancies up over 553%,
- Violent Crime up over 794%, and
- Public school SAT scores declined for over 18 straight years![24]

The United States of America is now the world leader in Abortion, Divorce, Teen Pregnancies, Illiteracy, Illegal Drugs and Violent Crimes, not to mention the disastrous economic price tag to an already out of control national budget.

God warned "in the last days perilous times shall come" (2 Timothy 3:1). But without a doubt the greatest peril to God and our Founders is that the nation that should have been the world's leading spiritual retardant of evil has now become one of its leading contributors!

Psalm 11:3 asks "If the foundations be destroyed, what can the righteous do", but reminds "The LORD is in His holy temple...His eyes behold, His eyelids try the children of men - The LORD trieth (but delivers) the righteous, but the wicked...His soul hateth (casts out)".

Again, Founder George Mason warned – "As nations cannot be rewarded or punished in the next world, so they must be in this; by an inevitable chain of causes and effects, Providence punishes national sins by national calamities"!

Is there any hope or remedy left for America?

Since as of this writing the Rapture has not yet occurred, based on America's Biblical Christian foundation and remaining remnant of faithful Biblical Christians and hopefully continued loyal alliance with Israel, this author is still prayerfully and Biblically convinced that God's sovereign answer is a resounding but conditional "YES" (see "God and Founders' 4-R's REMEDY VISION for America")!

But what are the chances today that America will experience great revival and national spiritual restoration? Only God knows for sure, but to have any chance God's churches must first be willing to meet His Biblical conditions for her own healing in order to fulfill His and Founders' vision of Remedy for the rest of America!

"Ye see the distress that we are in, Come, and let us (spiritually RESTORE)...that we be no more a reproach" (Nehemiah 2:17)!

*Chapter Five*

---

## GOD AND FOUNDERS' 4-R's
## REMEDY VISION FOR AMERICA:

### REPENTANCE Producing
### God-Pleaser Pastors

Is it even possible amidst our spiraling spiritual decay in these perilous last days to see prophetic people-pleaser pastors' passive permissiveness become prophetically-bold God-pleaser pastors and preachers in the pulpits of America's churches, in order to see spiritual restoration and a potential great harvest of souls come to Christ in America prior to His Rapture?

Upon their return to a demolished Jerusalem following their seventy year Babylonian captivity, God's prophet Nehemiah issued this prayerful but active challenge to Israel: "Ye see the distress that we are in, how Jerusalem lieth waste... Come and let us (spiritually restore), that we be no more a reproach" (Nehemiah 2:17), the theme verse for the prophetically empowered rare but divinely-needed ministry God has called me to!

In Ezekiel 22:30, God issued a chilling revelation "I sought for a man among them that should make up the hedge, and stand in the gap before Me for the land that I should not destroy it: but I found NONE – Therefore I have

poured out mine indignation upon them; I have consumed them with the fire of My wrath: their own way have I recompensed upon their heads, saith the Lord God"!

Today in America, God is looking for a "remnant of even one" prophetic God-pleaser pastor-preacher with Spirit-led boldness and courage to herald His call to REPENTANCE in confronting America's wickedness and apathy, starting in her churches and throughout our nation to rebuild her damaged spiritual foundation. The question is, are there any left like George Whitfield?

As a prophecy-gift pastor, God has led me to humbly and prayerfully strive to be such a pastor and evangelist, having been "democratically voted out" from two pastorates but still prayerfully open to remote possibility of leading a "remnant" church willing to endure sound doctrine.

So He called me as Founding-Evangelist of "God's Remedy For America" Evangelism Ministry, heralding His 4-R's Remedy VISION for any having "ear to hear" (Revelation 2:7):

1) Prayerful prophetic preaching producing genuine **REPENTANCE**, manifesting
2) Heaven-sent nationwide **REVIVAL** of His churches, motivating to
3) **REDISCOVERING** America's Republic, mobilizing to
4) **RESTORING** God in government by reclaiming right stance in the public arenas as Elijah [I KINGS 18] to evidence the fire of God and prayerfully see a GREAT HARVEST to CHRIST prior to His glorious return!

This vision tailored specifically to America's unique spiritual heritage but current spiritual condition is deeply rooted in God's prophetic four conditions for Israel (and even America and her churches today!) to receive His national forgiveness and healing – "If My people, which are called by My name, shall:

* **HUMBLE** themselves, and
* **PRAY**, and
* **SEEK** My face, and
* **TURN** (repent) from their wicked ways - then will I hear from heaven, and will forgive their sin, and will heal their land" (2 Chronicles 7:14).

Sadly today, America and even many of her churches are so filled with prideful ego in our own material prosperity and earthly accomplishment that we are largely living as though we do not need God anymore!

So God is prophetically but redemptively warning but reminding America and especially His churches today, "Despite your prideful arrogance, self-sufficiency and unrepentance, I love you and want to spare you the ultimate judgment and consequences of your condition if you'll only repent of your pride and humbly fall to your knees in prayer before Me"!

Scripturally, these steps of obedience especially apply to pastors to restore prophetically-empowered preaching and redemptively bold leadership in the pastorate. Each step of action becomes easier once the first is divinely accomplished, but the first step is often demonically most difficult!

*First*, prophetic people-pleaser pastors must brokenly humble ourselves of our prideful "need to succeed" which often leads us to "please men" in order to fulfill our fleshly desire for earthly spiritual status and recognition even in God's churches!

*Second*, we pastors must submissively go to God in prayer begging His forgiveness, as a prayer-less life is always a powerless life!

*Third*, we pastors must prayerfully seek God's face, and not His hand!

*Fourth* and most importantly, we pastors must repent (turn) from our men-pleasing ways and commit to primarily please God and not people, the very first word Jesus ever preached in Matthew 4:17. We must revisit our "professed" conversion, prayerfully asking God to Biblically reveal whether we are genuinely saved or just went through the motions!

We pastors must renounce and turn from our spiritual passivity and fear of men before God and commit to fear (reverence) only Christ! Perhaps the primary reason many pastors and leaders are so passively fearful and sin-tolerant today is because we may be outwardly religious like Nicodemus, but inwardly unregenerate!

It was Israel's own religious clergy of Sadducees, Scribes and Pharisees that feared Jesus most, afraid His divine power and mysteriously pure doctrine would shatter their comfortably privileged lifestyle of spiritual mastery over the people through their own man-made authority and traditions of men.

Like the Pharisees then, perhaps many pastors and religious leaders today enter the "ministry" not knowing Jesus at all, but simply opting for a perceived comfortable, privileged and lofty spiritual position or status to be looked up to in society – or maybe "mom or grandma" called us to ministry instead of God!

When Jesus replied to Nicodemus in John 3, He was speaking to one of the highest ranking and most well-respected ministers in the Jewish religious hierarchy. He was a member of the Sanhedrin (seventy elders and teachers of Israel), an expert of the Torah (Jewish Law) with vast liturgical knowledge, credential and experience!

But though outwardly very religious and perhaps occasionally even personally sincere in their beliefs, his dialogue with Jesus reveals these so-called "clergy members" were unregenerate and spiritually blind before Christ!

When Jesus declared His salvation mandate "Except a man be born again, he cannot see the kingdom of God" (John 3:3), Nicodemus' own response revealed this scholarly religious ruler's spiritual blindness, "How can a man be born when he is old? – can he enter the second time into his mother's womb and be born"? (John 3:4).

Nicodemus lacked spiritual eyesight to see even the most basic spiritual truth, as Jesus revealed his lost and blind spiritual condition by asking "Art thou a master of Israel, and knowest not these things"? (John 3:10).

Nicodemus was stunned by Jesus' words because being spiritually "born again" meant he would have to renounce all the systematic spiritual ladders he had climbed in life to get where he was, and be willing to start his spiritual journey all over again in Christ!

Apart from keeping the law or self-righteous ritual, he would have to repent and receive the love and forgiveness only Jesus could bring in order to be saved from his sin and become "reborn" into God's family, as even physical birth must be followed by the parents or adoptive parents' spiritual willingness to accept responsibility for an infant or child to inherit active family membership!

Like Nicodemus in that day, it is painfully probable that even most "religious leaders" today desperately need to experience this spiritual rebirth from above through Christ!

Jesus targeted His harshest criticism to the clergy within the temple because it was the spiritual leaders themselves whose hearts were farthest from Him, as He indicted their hypocrisy and false worship by declaring "(you) people draweth nigh unto me with (your) mouth and honoreth me with (your) lips, but (your) heart is far from me – in vain (you) do worship Me, teaching for doctrines the commandments of men" (Matthew 15:8-9).

In contrast to the lost Pharisees' fear of Jesus and though every unregenerate leader today still fears Jesus, even many saved pastors today often fear their congregations in the church since they see them as their source of support instead of God. Thus, their priority is often just to keep the people content by pleasing them, knowing their vocation will likely remain secure and comfortable in doing so.

Since most unregenerate pastors (and even some fearfully passive saved pastors) act like mere hirelings, they are usually willing to allow their followers and themselves to "enjoy the pleasures of sin for a season", given the immediate acceptance and success it often brings to them in their vocation. Pastors, if this describes you, Jesus lovingly but boldly implores you as He did Nicodemus to turn from your spiritual blindness and be born again into His family by praying a prayer such as this:

"Dear Lord, I know I am a sinner and cannot save myself - thank you for dying on the cross for my sins - I now repent of my sin and ask you to come into my heart Lord Jesus - forgive my sin and save my soul - I give you my life - make me the person you want me to be - in Jesus' name, AMEN"!

Having taken this simple but essential step of faith and as you begin your new life in Christ through prayer and His Word, you will slowly find your fear of man being replaced with a holy boldness and desire to lead others to Jesus no matter how unpopular it may be or what the personal cost, as Paul concluded "For I am not ashamed of the gospel of Christ, for it is the power of God unto salvation to every one that believeth" (Romans 1:16).

But if already genuinely saved, pastors who still continue to be weak and fearful leaders must pray for revival in their own hearts to overcome this fear and weakness, asking God for a holy boldness to confront sin as we revisit the empty cross to rediscover the resurrected Christ like the empowered Peter of Pentecost did!

If Jesus truly lives within us as born-again believers, perhaps along the way we have merely taken our eyes off of Jesus and lost vision of His power to overcome even death itself, which may explain why many have become so spiritually fearful of men. Proverbs 29:18 says "Where there is no VISION the people perish, but he that keepeth the law, happy is he"!

Even Israel's righteous King David, whom God declared "a man after my own heart" (I Samuel 13:14), confessed his grievous sins of adultery and murder against God - "Against thee and thee only have I sinned…I acknowledge my transgressions and my sin is ever before me…The sacrifices of God are a broken spirit and contrite heart, (which) thou wilt not despise" (Psalm 51:3,4,17).

When we come before God truly broken and repentant over our own failures and sins, He will not turn His ear from us but will mercifully forgive us, though some consequences of our sins may remain.

King David evidenced true repentance in two Biblically essential ways – first, he did not defend himself when confronted by Nathan the prophet (2 Samuel 12:13), and second, he was faithfully willing to humbly accept the consequences of his sins (Psalm 51:4).

Had America's White House contained such a president from 1992 to 2000 willing to clearly evidence genuine repentance to God in this way, then his personal forgiveness and even national healing and restoration could have been Biblically set in motion!

But God is looking for our nation's pastors to evidence true brokenness and genuine repentance in His churches by humbly "confessing" ("to speak with" or agree with God) about our sins and failures (I John 1:9), and be willing to personally accept His Biblical consequences, whatever they may be.

Perhaps a most obvious consequence many saved pastors have had to endure due to our failure to defend and preserve the bride's spiritual purity is simply having to daily contend with churches plagued by rampant disobedience and spiritual bondage to sin that threatens her very survival.

For prophetically passive people-pleaser pastors to become empowered with divine but redemptive boldness to confront sin, they must be willing to do exactly what Peter and John did in Acts 4:13 - spend daily quantity and quality time "with Jesus" through prayer and His Word!

Even most well-intentioned pastors today are either so encumbered with the daily needs of the church that they spend all their time trying to put out fires, or so comfortable spending time being recreationally entertained by congregation or fellowshipping at church breakfasts, dinners and fellowships, that they spend precious little or no time with Jesus in His Word and prayer!

Many churches expect pastors to faithfully feed the flock on Sunday, but rarely allow them needed time with Jesus. No wonder when the times of challenge or testing come, they often lack boldness and courage to stand up against sin and rebuke it.

Every pastor must make it his top priority to spend much quality time with Jesus meditating in His Word and following His ways if he is going to have spiritual courage and resolve in his time of testing!

His life must be characterized by faithful prayer, since a prayer-filled life is a power-filled life! He must daily seek to be conformed to Christ as he meditates on His Word. He must daily worship Jesus in spirit and in truth, knowing He alone is worthy of our praise and adoration, possessing all power to do all things we cannot do ourselves. He must fall in love with Jesus afresh and anew each day so that Jesus' perfect love casts out all fear of man!

Satan will predictably present many daily distractions and alternatives vying for our time and attention, but the pastor who faithfully spends his time daily experiencing the resurrected Christ will have a holy boldness and courage about him to face any difficulty or challenge the enemy throws his way, knowing that because Jesus overcame death itself, "we are more than conquerors through Him that loved us" (Romans 8:37)!

This is what transformed the "prophetically passive" Peter prior to Pentecost into the prophetically bold and empowered Peter of Pentecost! Praise God this same power of the resurrected Christ can radically transform even the most passive people-pleaser pastors today into the most prophetic God-pleaser pastors and preachers this generation has ever seen, with the holy boldness and courage to proclaim truth and expose sin through the redemptive power of Christ regardless of personal price!

Even in Ezekiel's day amongst the nation of Israel, God said "I sought for a man among them, that should make up the hedge, and stand in the gap before me for the land, that I should not destroy it: but I found none" (Ezekiel 22:30).

Is there any doubt God is diligently searching for such men of boldness and courage today, willing to boldly and courageously stand in the gap before God for a lost and dying nation and world by refusing to accept and fiercely combat Satan's influence over our culture's wicked living both inside and outside the church?

Even in America today, God has always had a remnant willing to endure the sound doctrine that people-pleaser pastors and sin-thetic sheep today disdain, willing to have their spiritual toes boldly but lovingly and redemptively stepped on by prophetic God-pleaser pastors (see "REVIVAL Awakening Authentic Sheep")!

"Almighty God, please raise up such men starting with me, prophetic God-pleaser pastors and church leaders in our adulterous generation empowered with the holy boldness and courage to proclaim your truth and redemptively expose sin with no concern for self-preservation in the face of an often hostile nation and even church!

May we humbly but boldly lead your churches and sheep to faithfully fulfill the second condition in your 4-R's Remedy VISION to receive your divine forgiveness and spiritual healing for our nation and even potentially reap a great harvest of souls to Christ in America before everlasting too late – in Jesus' name, AMEN"!

---

## Chapter Six

REVIVAL Awakening Authentic Sheep

Is there any hope for America and her churches today? Can God really awaken and REVIVE His "sleeping giant" the church and even our beloved nation?

Having preached evangelistic revivals in America's churches and even spoken in many secular patriotic organizations, the "majority consensus" seems to think not! But "With men this is impossible, but with God all things (even hope for America!) are possible" (Matthew 19:26)!

God's remedy does not begin in our schools, businesses or even government, "For the time is come that judgment must begin at the house of God: and if it first begin at us, what shall the end be of them that obey not the gospel of God" I Peter 4:17?

Once again, His conditional blueprint starts with His people the church:

"IF My people, which are called by My name, shall humble themselves and pray, and seek My face (not My hand), and turn (repent) from their wicked ways; then will I hear from heaven, and will forgive their sin, and will heal their land" (2 Chronicles 7:14)!

Can we actually begin to see sin-thetic straying sheep become and act like authentic sheep? Before addressing this question, we should first understand how real sheep-herders of the pastures deal with this problem!

Jesus said the wolves and goats would always be present to prey upon or disrupt the flock, cautioning His submissive sheep to be "wise as serpents and harmless as doves" (Matthew 10:16). But every real sheep-herder knows that one "straying sheep" can do almost as much harm to the flock as the wolves and goats by influencing the entire flock to leave the shepherd and venture into unprotected paths of destruction!

This is why actual sheep-herders will often reluctantly "sacrifice" a most prized and beautiful "straying" sheep to protect the rest of the flock from its destructive influence simply by ignoring this imperiled stray. Naturally, this regretful final option is carried out only IF the shepherd's exhaustive efforts in training the straying sheep to heed his voice with his gentle shepherd's nook have proved futile.

Amusingly enough, no doubt a remnant of godly under-shepherds in the church have perhaps jokingly wished there was a Biblically permissible way to "actively sacrifice" a sin-thetic straying sheep from the flock, but God's way is to passively but mournfully ignore this unrepentant stray!

As Romans 8:13 reveals, God's often terminal judgment for habitually straying from the shepherd is identical to the sheep-herder who must "sacrifice" his straying sheep. When sin-thetic habitual straying sheep continually refuse to heed the warning to follow the shepherd, God's submissive sheep are wise to "steer clear" of this straying sheep at all costs, because certain danger or even physical death may follow him!

But as long as there is an ounce of breath left in these sin-thetic straying sheep, thank God there is the same hope for them as for people-pleaser pastors and all sinners in the world – "Repent, for the kingdom of heaven is at hand" (Matthew 4:17)!

Since many sin-thetic sheep may be known by God to be lost sheep (Matthew 7:21), they desperately need to be saved so Jesus can help them to stop straying and follow Him. They must turn one hundred eighty degrees from their sinful self-will and ask Jesus to come into their heart and take control of their life as they begin submissively following the Great Shepherd!

Then this formerly lost straying sheep who was determined to influence his own life and others will begin to be filled with a desire to follow the Great Shepherd's voice. No longer will he want to rebel against the Good Shepherd's authority or even His faithful under-shepherds, but begins to hunger to submit to God and His ordained leadership. Then he can sincerely begin to pray as Christ, "Not my will, but thine be done" (Luke 22:42).

But just like people-pleaser pastors, making sure of salvation must be followed by the daily discipline of spending time with Jesus through prayer and in His Word. This newly submissive sheep will want to daily strive to be conformed to Christ by saturating his mind and heart with Jesus' words and ways!

This discipline will mean that many of his former fleshly habits and time expenditures (example, television, hobbies, entertainments and worldly pursuits) will desire to be reduced or even discarded and replaced with prayer, God's Word, faithful worship and witnessing for Jesus!

In order to "practice" submission, sin-thetic straying sheep will need to replace their thoughts, opinions and attitudes derived from many worldly sources with the thoughts of Christ through His Word. The great apostle Paul admonished Christ's submissive sheep to "bring every thought captive to the obedience of Christ " (2 Corinthians 10:5), knowing that "as (a man) thinketh in his heart, so is he" (Proverbs 23:7)! Christ must be allowed to "sanctify and cleanse it (our heart and mind) with the washing of water by the Word" (Ephesians 5:26).

Once this process of submission to Christ has begun, it will naturally evidence itself by a new-found genuine desire to faithfully follow the Biblical counsel of prophetically-empowered God-pleaser pastors in the church!

Though these former "straying sheep" may not yet fully comprehend the spiritual principles of God's Word at work in his life or the church, as he grows in the grace of God's Word, the Spirit of Christ will help him submissively follow Biblical counsel instead of selfishly straying from the shepherd!

IF a sin-thetic straying sheep in the church is already genuinely saved but continues to habitually stray from the Great Shepherd, the remedy for this problem is usually more challenging, including Matthew 18 church discipline and perhaps even including God's mortal judgment in cases of the genuinely saved continuing in their unrepentance (Romans 8:13).

But in most churches, comparatively little time or attention is usually offered to help such Christians wage "spiritual warfare" to take back the ground we yielded to Satan. Since the thought of warfare usually has little appeal to us even as Christians, we often subtly resign ourselves to be mastered by the same old sins we were enslaved by before Christ. The explanation we offer for this is usually "that's just the way I am", "you can't teach an old dog new tricks", or "I get it from my parents". Though these feeble excuses may seem innocent and humorous, they usually indicate strong evidence there remains in our lives ground and strongholds yielded to and built by the enemy.

Paul cautions us "give no place (ground) to the devil" (Ephesians 4:27)!

We give ground to Satan when we entertain and ultimately yield to his temptations. The more we yield to a particular sin, the more ground we give to him in that area. When he secures enough ground through our habitual sin pattern, he immediately and systematically begins to build a stronghold (fortress) on his stolen property.

Once construction of the stronghold is complete, not only are lost people obviously powerless to free themselves from this bondage, but even many Christians may feel overwhelmed by the spiritual reality of this lingering pre-salvation imprisonment and resign in defeat to these strongholds which had conquered them prior to salvation.

The Bible offers at least five prayerful steps of spiritual warfare a Christian must take to bind and rebuke Satan in "Reclaiming Surrendered Ground" to the pulling down of spiritual strongholds in order to experience victory and freedom through Christ,[25] as Paul declared "For we wrestle not against flesh and blood, but against principalities and powers, against the rulers of the darkness of this world, against spiritual wickedness in high places" (Ephesians 6:12)!

In 2 Corinthians 10:4 he went on to reveal "For the weapons of our warfare are not carnal, but mighty through God to the pulling down of strongholds – casting down every high thing that exalteth itself against the knowledge of God, and bringing into captivity every thought to the obedience of Christ"!

These spiritually liberating steps can be applied to any area we may be imprisoned by, including Satan's primary areas of attack like pride, rebellion, occult activity, sexual immorality, bitterness, disobedience, stubbornness and unforgiveness. Other common areas are anger, worry, depression, jealousy, physical and mental addiction, guilt, habits, doubt and fear, to name a few!

The first action step is almost the same initial step necessary for salvation – we must genuinely repent or turn from our sin, as Jesus declared "Repent, for the kingdom of heaven is at hand" (Matthew 4:17).

Through the power of His Holy Spirit we must stop using God's grace as a license to continue committing the same sin and be willing to allow Him to radically change our direction by turning our back on the sin and choosing to obey and follow Jesus. If we genuinely ask His forgiveness and truly repent, Jesus will forgive and if allowed help us in this process to take the next step!

Second, we must be willing to take back the spiritual ground we foolishly yielded to Satan, as Paul said "Let him that stole steal no more" (Ephesians 4:28)!

Since we ourselves passively gave this ground to the enemy, with Christ's help we are the ones who must decide to boldly stand up to this spiritual bully and courageously take it back, as John reminds us "Greater is He that is in you than he that is in the world" (I John 4:4)!

James further declared "Submit your selves to God, resist the devil and he will flee from you"(James 4:7). Once a parcel of ground has been taken back by confronting the enemy through Christ, it allows Jesus to accomplish the next step!

Third, since Satan is the one who built the stronghold fortress, Jesus is the only one who can tear down the stronghold, but we must prayerfully ask Him to do so! Paul said "For the weapons of our warfare are not carnal, but mighty through God to the pulling down of strongholds" (2 Corinthians 10:4). Since no physical structure can be erected without land to build on, once you have prayerfully taken back the ground, simply prayerfully ask Jesus to tear down the enemy's castle and He will faithfully collapse it!

Fourth, we must begin to build towers of truth in our life through His Word to fill the vacuum of space created by the demolished stronghold. Jesus said "Ye shall know the truth, and the truth shall make you free" (John 8:32)!

Since Satan was allowed the ground to build the stronghold through lies and deception, we must begin replacing his lies with God's truth, or else the enemy will ultimately pierce this newly created vacuum and refill it with the same lies and deception we started with, only stronger!

Fifth, we must diligently begin to bring our every thought captive to Christ. Paul said "Casting down imaginations and every high thing that exalteth itself against the knowledge of God, and bringing into captivity every thought to the obedience of Christ" (2 Corinthians 10:5).

Since every sin we ultimately commit originated with a mere thought, we must learn to exclusively allow only the thoughts of Christ and His Word to control our minds and hearts, since we have already seen that "As (a man) thinketh in his heart, so is he" (Proverbs 23:7).

By faith, once a true Christian genuinely takes and practices these scriptural steps in his daily life, he can begin to experience true and lasting victory over the power of sin which caused him to stray in the first place!

Once this now submissive sheep practices faithful obedience to the Great Shepherd, this former sin-thetic sheep will have little problem placing himself under the protective authority and leadership of His prophetically-empowered godly pastor in the church!

Though Jesus reveals that the majority of people will prophetically remain lost or straying sheep, in these last days may those having "ear to hear" (Revelation 2:7) obey Christ through His godly prophetic pastors in remnant churches to "follow Jesus as fishers of men" (Matthew 4:19), actively seeking to save the lost while there is still time!

We must not let the majority's rejection and disobedience against Christ discourage us from following Him and do all we can to lead other lost sheep to Jesus, since ultimately we will give account only for ourselves and not for others!

"Heavenly Father, please forgive your church and leaders for disobediently allowing ourselves to become vessels of self-fulfillment of perilous prophecy through apathetic conformity to a lost world. We beg Your mercy and grace as we repent of our wicked ways and return to

89

our first love, helping restore America's spiritual foundation –

May we your Bride readily repent and receive your cleansing touch so that Jesus may once again present her a glorious church in position and even endeavoring in practice without spot or wrinkle, but holy and without blemish -

Create in (us) a clean heart O Lord, and renew a right spirit within us – restore unto us the joy of thy salvation – then will we teach transgressors thy ways and sinners shall be converted unto thee -

Amidst a wicked, disobedience and adulterous generation driven by our own fleshly passions, may the Bridegroom return to find a repentant bride pure and set apart from sin to please her Righteous and Faithful Groom by obediently following Him as faithful fishers of men to offer Your salvation to a lost and dying nation and world! -

But even as many tragically reject Christ and forever perish in their sins, we pray You would find our hands unstained by their blood by faithfully issuing Your loving but bold warning of the impending eternal agony, torment and separation awaiting unrepentant hearts – in Jesus' name, Amen"!

America's now hopefully prophetically empowered pastors and authentic revived sheep surely are wise to hear and heed God's exhortations for repentance and revival, anointing and motivating her to lead individuals to Christ once again! So isn't this enough - do churches really need to get "mixed up in national politics"? God's (and our Founders') answer is simple but profound!

Today's church vision is often "micro-man" sized instead of "macro-Messiah" sized! Thus Christians and churches are often content to win a single soul to Christ, since Jesus exhorts us to "leave the ninety and nine and go after that which is lost, until he find it" (Luke 15:4), evidencing the eternal value of every individual soul to God! Thus each true Christian should faithfully evidence this by personally following Jesus as fishers of individual souls!

But the Bible also says God is "not willing that any should perish, but that all should come to repentance" (2 Peter 3:9)!

God's divine desire is for all people to repent and come to Christ! But since "wide is the gate and broad is the way that leadeth to destruction, and many there be which go in thereat" (Matthew 7:13), due to the hardness of human hearts He prophetically knows most will not repent since "strait is the gate and narrow is the way which leadeth unto life, and few there be that find it" (Matthew 7:14)!

But if America's churches will embrace His "macro-Messiah" sized vision for souls, she will long for and endeavor to see a great harvest of souls come to Christ in America!

But for this to happen, His churches must prayerfully fulfill the third step of His specific 4-R's REMEDY VISION for America's unique spiritual foundation and form of government in order to meet His conditions for national forgiveness and healing!

## Chapter Seven

---

## REDISCOVERING America's Republic!

Was America really established as a Republic and not a democracy? What official national documentation did America's Founders evidence as proof? Exactly what is a Republic according to Founders and what is the primary difference between a Republic and a democracy? Why is this difference so Divinely crucial to America's survival as a Republic and nation?

Furthermore, is America really a "Christian nation" and if so, how could our Founders have established her as such without violating their First Amendment?

As we will see, though much of America today seems to have forgotten the once common knowledge that most of her Founders, though surely not perfect men faithfully endeavored to embrace Biblical Christian principles, willing to sacrifice "their lives, fortunes and sacred honor" (Declaration of Independence) to establish our beloved nation, as it is divinely imperative for all true active patriots to REDISCOVER our spiritual identity, or passively allow Founders' divinely-unique form of government to cease "practice" on earth!

As per book title, it is paramount to realize that our faithful Founders did not just "dream up" their idea
of our Republic, the only nation in world history to

remain under one form of government for well over two centuries, but as we will see our Founders got the overwhelming "majority" of their foundational principles directly or indirectly from God!

Our Founders' answer to our first question "Was America really established as a Republic and not a democracy?" is clearly documented, wisely evidencing that they based the "operation" of our Republic's Constitution (according to Article 7) upon their profound God-referencing document of divine principle (Declaration of Independence),[26] applying God's principle "Blessed is the nation whose God is the LORD" (Psalm 33:12)!

That is why Article 4-Section 4: Constitution officially states: "The United States shall guarantee to every state in this Union a republican form of government"!

Another official national document, our Pledge of Allegiance clearly reaffirms America's identity as nation as we pledge to the "Republic for which it stands", not the democracy for which it stands, as our Founders were not referring to a political party, but to the most divinely unique form of government in world history!

The vast "majority" of our Founders adhered to Christian principles, as evidenced by their official founding document, our Declaration of Independence's four synonymous references to "God...the Supreme Judge of the world", with thirty-four percent of Founders' quotes based directly on the Bible and sixty percent from authors who based their writings on Scripture![27]

93

Thus ninety four percent of our Founders' quotes were based either directly or indirectly upon the Bible! Consider just the following micro-sample:

"The Bible is the chief moral cause of all that is good and the best corrector of all that is evil in human society – the best book for regulating the temporal concerns of men"
– Founder Noah Webster[28]

"I have examined all religions, and the result is that the Bible is the best book in the world"
– Founder President John Adams[29]

"Reason and experience both forbid us to expect that national morality can prevail in exclusion of religious principle"
– George Washington[30]

"The precepts of philosophy laid hold of actions only, but Jesus pushed His scrutinies into the heart of man, erected His tribunal in the region of his thoughts, and purified the waters at the fountainhead"
– Founder President Thomas Jefferson[31]

"By renouncing the Bible, philosophers swing from their moorings upon all moral subjects – It is the only correct map of the human heart that ever has been published"
- Founder Benjamin Rush[32]

Today, "non-patriots" of our Republic as previously revealed in Washington's Final Farewell Address (Myth of Demonic "Democracy") are quick to point out that our Founders' quotes are not "official" national documents.

As we will see however, our Founders' quotes stating our Republic's source of authority as the Bible support their official national documents declaring our Republican form of government.

Proponents of democracy use a historically profound but not official national document, claiming Lincoln's Gettysburg Address phrase "of the people, by the people, for the people" refers to democracy! But as we will see, Lincoln's "unofficial" address is actually consistent with his chosen Republican party-affiliation!

In fact, not one official founding document ever mentions the words "democracy or democratic"! In any legally-objective court of law, the indisputable legal documentation evidences that our Republic is irrefutably victorious over democracy - TWO (Constitution and Pledge of Allegiance) versus ZERO!

In fact, many today do not even realize the Bible served as our Founders' foundational source of most of their principles for operating our Republic, including the "Three Branches of Government" (Legislative, Executive, Judicial – Isaiah 33:22), "Tax Exempt Status of Churches" (Ezra 7:24) and "Separation of POWERS" (Jeremiah 7:24), [33] just to name a few!

In 1892, America's Supreme Court noted that each of the forty-four states then in our union had some type of God-centered declaration charging profound spiritual requirements for candidates to even hold government office! [34] For example:

"Every person appointed to public office shall say 'I do profess faith in God the Father, and in Jesus Christ His only Son, and in the Holy Ghost, one God blessed for evermore, and I do acknowledge the Holy Scriptures of the Old and New Testaments to be given by Divine Inspiration"
– Delaware Constitution (1776)![35]

"No person who shall deny the being of God, or the truth of the Christian religion, or the divine authority of the Old or New Testaments, or who shall hold religious principles incompatible with the freedom and safety of the state, shall be capable of holding any office, or place of trust or profit in the civil department, within this state"
– North Carolina Constitution (1776)![36]

But exactly what is a Republic and why is her preservation of primary importance to America's survival as a nation?

According to Webster's Dictionary, a republic is a "public thing, state or government, specifically one headed by a president, in which the power is exercised through officials representing the voters who elected them".

Our Founders gave us the most divine form of government in world history, combining a representative form of government with Divine responsibility and accountability, in which its citizens wisely elect "statesmen" (not "politicians" - BELOW) to represent and exercise authority on their behalf, then holding their statesmen earthly accountable for their decisions, these statesmen embracing their eternal accountability before God!

But according to our Founders, the primary difference between America's divinely unique Republic and a simple democracy which explains her over two century endurance is her Source of Authority! Consider what our authoritative Founders declared and evidenced:

Founder Noah Webster stated "Our citizens should early understand that THE genuine source of correct republican principles is the BIBLE"![37]

Founder Benjamin Rush put it this way – "The ONLY means of establishing and perpetuating our republican form of government is the universal education of our youth in the principles of Christianity by means of the BIBLE"![38]

And as previously noted, Noah Webster stated "The BIBLE is the chief moral cause of all that is good and the best corrector of all that is evil in human society – the best book for regulating the temporal concerns of men", and John Adams testified "I have examined all religions, and the result is that the BIBLE is the best book in the world"!

According to America's Founders, our Republic is a representative form of government whose sole source of authority is the Bible, acknowledging Israel's and Christianity's God of the Bible as her only source of authority for our Republic!

Thus in our Republic, each citizen enjoys equal voting privilege as in a democracy, but her very survival depends on each voter fulfilling his grave responsibility to align his vote with the Bible by electing statesmen whose voting records align with Scripture, with the firm understanding that each voter will ultimately stand alone before "God the

Supreme Judge of the world" to give account for himself and his decisions affecting the nation!

Thus for America's Republic to be preserved, it is divinely imperative that her citizens faithfully uphold Biblical principle in their voting decisions and actions, which is why when Founder Benjamin Franklin was asked:

"What have you given us"? - he prophetically replied, "A Republic, IF you can keep it"![39]

Accordingly, John Adams also declared "We have no government armed with power capable of contending with human passions unbridled by morality and religion"![40]

In fact, a most profound and intriguing discourse over how to best ensure good government was engaged in by two notable leaders well before independence from England was established! Consider:

John Locke, the author of the 1669 Carolina Constitution believed good government is secured solely through enactment of good laws. Locke reasoned that if righteous laws were in the Constitution, then no matter who was placed into office, he would always be bound by those righteous laws.[41]

But William Penn, the establisher of the government of Pennsylvania applied a dramatically different philosophy! While Penn surely agreed with Locke that good laws were divinely essential to the preservation of our Republic, he did not believe a long state constitution filled with righteous laws could ever guarantee good government – Penn explained:

"Government, like clocks, go from the motion men give them – Wherefore governments rather depend upon men, than men upon governments – let men be good and the government cannot be bad – but if men be bad, the government will never be good. I know some say, let us have good laws, and no matter for the men that execute them – But let them consider that though good laws do well, good men do better – for good laws may lack good men – but good men will never lack good laws, nor allow bad ones"![42]

Thus our Founders defined and personally endeavored to embody the profound difference between a statesman and a mere "politician", realizing the primary key to good government is found not only in the quality of laws which are passed, though good Biblical laws are essential to preservation of Republic, but in the quality of the people who govern based on Proverbs 29:2:

"When the righteous are in authority the people rejoice, but when the wicked beareth rule the people mourn"!

According to our Founders, a "politician" is someone who would "compromise public principle to advance his own interests", which America's recent history reveals far too many of today - but a statesman is someone who "would not compromise public principle, but embraces the Biblical conviction of future reward and punishment",[43] which America seemingly has far too few of today!

John Adams further evidenced the divine essentiality of statesmen and people of faith to preserve our Republic when he said, "Our Constitution was made only for a moral and religious people – it is wholly inadequate to the government of any other"![44]

Remember the example in Myth of Demonic "Democracy" where the "majority ruled" in the hypothetical vote to legalize murder? But in a faithfully practicing Republic, murder (the killing of innocent life) is always a crime (sin) because it is always prohibited by our Republic's source of authority, the Bible (Exodus 20:13)!

But as strongly contested as these questions are in America today, the next one is where the spiritual warfare supernaturally intensifies! Is America really a Christian nation and if so, how could our Founders establish her as such without violating First Amendment?

Once again our Founders' Declaration of Independence and Constitution [Article 4 -Section 4], supported by their wise writings officially evidence their answer to these crucial questions:

George Washington declared "You do well to wish to learn our arts and ways of life, and above all the religion of Jesus Christ - these will make you a greater and happier people than you are"![45]

Founder John Witherspoon testified "There is no salvation in any other than in Jesus Christ of Nazareth"![46]

Thus John Adams collaborated with fellow-Founder John Hancock to profoundly declare for our Republic, "We recognize no sovereign but God, and no king but Jesus"![47]

Founder Noah Webster declared "The Christian religion is the basis and source of all genuine freedom in government; I am persuaded that no civil government of a republican form can exist and be durable in which the principles of Christianity have not a controlling influence"![48]

Thomas Jefferson (then rumored to be a "Deist") further testified, "I am a real Christian – that is to say, a disciple of the doctrines of Jesus Christ"![49]

John Adams further declared "The general principles on which the fathers achieved independence were the general principles of Christianity"![50]

Founder and Fourth Chief-Justice of Supreme Court John Marshall stated "With us, Christianity and religion are identified. It would be strange indeed if with such a people our institutions did not presuppose Christianity and did not often refer to it and exhibit relations with it"![51]

Founder-First Chief Justice-Supreme Court John Jay declared "Providence (God) has given to our people the choice of their rulers, and it is the duty as well as the privilege and interest of our Christian nation to select and prefer Christians for their rulers"![52]

When is the last time America has heard such "politically incorrect" things from her Supreme Court? It was no coincidence that Chief-Justice Jay's profound declaration closely aligned with and was directly based on Proverbs 29:2, "When the righteous are in authority the people rejoice, but when the wicked beareth rule the people mourn"!

Our Founders primarily got their ideas for America's Republic directly or indirectly from Israel's God of the Bible! Spiritually according to God, there are two types of people in the world - the righteous and the wicked, the spiritually lost and the spiritually saved, the non-Christian and

101

the Christian, as Jesus said "He that is not with Me is against Me, and he that gathereth not with Me scattereth abroad" (Matthew 12:30)!

According to our Founders, America was indeed founded as a general "non-denomination-sanctioned" Christian nation which, according to their official First Amendment intent previously revealed (Myth of "Separation of Church and State") obviously did not violate their prohibition of a federally-sanctioned denomination of Christianity!

In fact, true Christianity is not a mere religion or denomination, but purely a voluntary personal spiritual relationship with Christ!

Mere religion is man's futile way of trying to reach God, which is why there are so many world "religions" today! But Christianity is God's way of reaching down to do for sinful mankind what we could not do for ourselves - spiritually save us from our sin as Jesus said "For the Son of man is come to seek and to save that which was lost" (Luke 19:10).

Thus when the Founders' of our Christian Republic referred to "religion", their own writings evidence they were referring to solely Bible-based religions. Does this mean that everyone in America is a true Christian? Obviously but sadly not, though Biblically America would obviously be in better though surely not perfect spiritual condition if we all truly knew and faithfully endeavored to act like the Christ of Christianity!

But it does mean that our Founders' established America as a Bible-based Christian Republic whose sole source of authority is the Bible, as the "majority" of our Founders naturally applied their personal relationship with Christ in molding and shaping our beloved nation, praying future generations to faithfully preserve our Republic by voting Biblically!

Our Founders surely realized that Christianity is a voluntary and deeply personal decision which cannot be forced on anyone, spiritually transcending the notion of many "coercive national religions" throughout the world, since true Christianity is not mere religion or church denomination, but a divinely personal "born again" (John 3:3) relationship with Christ through simple repentance and faith in Him alone!

What our faithful Founders were profoundly offering to the world was the opportunity to voluntarily choose the political earthly freedoms offered in our albeit "imperfectly implemented" Bible-based Christian Republic, and even voluntary eternal spiritual salvation offered through a personal relationship with the Christ of our general Christian Republic!

Thus the general vision of our Founders was to graciously but lawfully welcome to America anyone longing to flee the political peril and/or persecution of their native nation's forced "religion", and offer them divine opportunity to merely generically embrace the Bible and its political and spiritual freedoms in America's "non-denomination-sanctioned" Christian Republic - or simply exercise their God-given right to reject and leave.

Thus, our Founders' clearly documented that their definition of "freedom of religion" refers to freedom of any Bible-based religion or denomination of Christianity in order to help faithfully preserve our Bible-based Christian Republic!

Compare this to many other nations throughout world history who not only require an individual to officially swear allegiance to their national religion, but once within its borders not only forfeit their freedom to change their mind, but risk grave persecution or even death for being a "traitor or infidel"!

When our Founders established America as a solely Bible-based Republic, it was never their vision to violate God's First Commandment "Thou shalt have no other gods before Me" (Exodus 20:3) by "pluralistically embracing other gods", a tragic sin we have committed especially in recent decades, revealing why America now finds herself harboring many "other gods", even passively allowing erection of religious edifices worshiping many non-Biblical false gods under the myth of "freedom of any religion".

Hence for decades and especially since September 11 2001, America now finds herself enduring many tragic consequences for "having other gods", now trying to oppose a prophetic "wild man" (Ishmael and descendants - Genesis 16:12) passively accepted from within as citizens in our Republic, despite their prophetic intent to destroy Israel and her allies (Genesis 16:11), a most dangerous military challenge for our national security!

This is virtually the same tragic sin committed by Israel regarding God's fore-warned spiritual danger of embracing false Canaanite gods prophetically leading to her seventy year Babylonian Captivity, as God warned through Joshua "Come not among these nations, these that remain among you; neither make mention of the name of their gods, nor cause to swear by them, neither serve them, nor bow yourselves unto them" (Joshua 23:7).

But since we already have these "other gods" present as citizens within our midst, even many genuinely conservative American patriots may sadly wonder whether anything can be done toward possible remedy of this seemingly irreversible consequence of America's violation of God's First Commandment?

God and our Founders' likely reply to this question in America today is so divinely "politically-incorrect" that even some pastors and churches cringe to suggest that America return to our Biblical foundation by graciously allowing current citizens of other gods to maintain citizenship if they choose, while disallowing further erection of non-Bible-based religious edifices, then present future aspiring immigrants the purely voluntary opportunity to "generically" embrace the Bible of America's non-denomination-sanctioned Christian Republic, or freely exercise their God-given right to reject and depart.

Prophetically, the God of our Bible-based Republic promises He will "bless them that bless Israel, and curse him that curseth Israel" (Genesis 12:3). This is obviously one divinely important reason why God has historically blessed America as He has for her faithful support of His chosen Covenant people. But the primary reason is our

Founders' Biblical foundation for our Christian Republic, which divinely instructs us to bless Israel!

Leaving this now "politically incorrect" subject and at God's instruction, we must also address another politically-incorrect issue in our practicing democracy today – consider:

1960 marked the first time in our history that America elected a President of a religion officially claiming additional sources of authority to the Bible (Pope-Vatican).[53] This fact gravely contradicted our Founders' solely Bible-based Republic, which is historically and clearly evident.

In 2012, even a so-called "Republican" Presidential candidate embraced a religion which also claims sources of authority in addition to the Bible ("Book of Mormon, Pearl of Great Price, Doctrine and Covenants").[54] It is clearly evident this also gravely contradicts our Founders' solely Bible-based Republic.

But in 2008, a far more subtle scenario unfolded in America requiring much deeper diligence to divinely discern the spiritual identity of her White House occupant. During his first-term candidacy and Presidency, this particular politician was long-affiliated with a historically "mainline Christian church" led by a highly controversial pastor in Chicago, Illinois.

Throughout this church's history, she had formally claimed the Bible as her sole source of authority – that is until 1968.

Following Reverend Martin Luther King's tragic assassination, an influx of radical black Muslims whose source of authority is the "Quran" began to headquarter in Chicago, teaching that it was "impossible to be both black and Christian". Accordingly convinced by the demonic deceiver, this "church" then sought to "re-contextualize Christianity through Black Liberation Theology".[55]

Though his public voting record evidences vast violations of the Bible especially on the crucial moral and spiritual issues of abortion and sodomy, this President successfully influenced many in our Founders' solely Bible-based Republic to perceive him as a "politically-correct Christian", further evidencing America's degeneration into a practicing demonic democracy, virtually forgetting her true spiritual identity.

Today, even many "conservative American patriots" often assume that even our most ungodly voters are "loyal dedicated patriotic Americans too, but just happen to have different opinions to which they are politically entitled in our democracy"!

But remember George Washington's definition of an actual non-patriot? - "Of all the dispositions and habits which lead to political prosperity, religion and morality are indispensable supports; in vain would that man claim the tribute of patriotism who should labor to subvert these great pillars"!

According to the "Father of our Nation", any citizen or public leader regardless of political party, whose agenda is to "subvert (undermine) these great pillars" (Bible-based religion and morality) not only cannot claim to be a patriot, but has actually evidenced himself a traitor to America's Republic by endeavoring to undermine the very foun-

107

dations of her spiritual survival and blessing.

But it is also reproachfully essential to address an intense historical blight even in America's Republic - the grave sin of slavery and its cross-generational injustice in America! The liberal proponents of democracy routinely use their racially-charged argument "You cannot vote for Republicans because her Founders were slave owners" in effort to condition a divinely important citizen group of our nation to reject our Founders' Bible-based Republic in order to support demonically subjective majority-rule democracy.

The God of the Bible condemns the sin of forced servitude against any human being, as His mission is spiritually transforming people to be set free from our bondage and slavery to sin (John 8:32) to voluntarily serve Jesus Christ as redemptive Lord! While Scripture documents the obvious historical presence of forced slavery in our fallen world, it never condones it but sternly warns Christians, "And do the same (good) things unto servants, knowing that your Master also is in heaven; neither is there respect (preference) of persons with Him" (Ephesians 6:9)!

Throughout the history of sinful man, there has and tragically always will be the plague of powerful people oppressing or enslaving the weak for many reasons motivated by the "love of money...the root of all evil" (I Timothy 6:10)– just ask God's Israelites after four hundred years of bondage in Egypt! In fact even in today's world, it is sadly estimated that over twelve million people are still under some form of forced bondage and slavery![56]

History reveals that a few of the Founders indeed had slaves, as did many "democrats" in America, facts strategically used or silenced today in attempt to repel a most significant portion of our beloved population against America's Founders and Republic!

But today's proponents of democracy also conveniently fail to mention that our Founders clearly understood that slavery was a deep plague of national reproach, as some like George Washington even freed or treated them with daily compassion and mercy, as a Founder's son (John Quincy Adams) became known as the "Hell-Hound of Slavery" for his long years' effort of "dogged" determination in Congress to abolish it, while most Founders regretfully realized it was such a deep moral, social and spiritual plague that it likely would not see eradication in their lifetime or possibly even the century beyond.

This is why it is no mere coincidence that "four score and seven years" later a valiant proponent of our Bible-based Republic and author of the Gettysburg Address became known as the "Great Emancipator" (Abraham Lincoln), the vessel God would divinely use to help begin the slow and painful process toward His goal of national repentance from this grave iniquity!

Thus amongst true Christian patriots of our Founders' Bible-based Republic today, our disapproval for any candidate must never be based upon outer "skin", but upon a wicked inward heart evidenced by a sinful un-Biblical voting record which, according to George Washington demonically "subverts the great pillars" of America's Republic!

But today in America, it is Biblically essential to spiritually confront one more satanically strategic effort by demonic democracy's proponents who subtly suggest that those who commit the crime of sodomy should be entitled to the same "civil rights" that our African-American citizens were long sinfully denied for innocently being born black!

Obviously the God of the Bible unconditionally loves all people in the world including sodomites (John 3:16)! But His forgiveness of sin, no matter who commits it or how seemingly big or small, is conditioned upon genuine repentance and faith in God through His Son Jesus Christ!

Scripture very "politically-incorrectly" declares this grave iniquity an "abomination" (Leviticus 18:22) and "vile affections...who changed the truth of God into a lie...(so) God gave them over to a reprobate mind...receiving in themselves that recompense of their error which was meet" (Romans 1:25-28).

Prior to 1962 for almost two centuries in our Bible-based Republic, the sin of sodomy was legally classified a "crime-against-nature felony in every state, punishable by a lengthy term of imprisonment and/or hard labor".[57]

But today's proponents of democracy routinely slander America's African-American population by equating blacks' Biblically-affirmed struggle for civil rights with the abominable sin of sodomy, evidencing that contrary to public reputation, proponents of demonic democracy apparently believe being born black is an abominable sin just like sodomy!

What an amazing prejudice and discrimination against America's black citizens, yet demonic democrats systematically accuse all Republicans as racial bigots!

Finally and quite predictably today, proponents of demonic democracy now hatefully label supporters of our Founders' Bible-based Christian Republic as the "radical religious right", strategically and routinely categorizing us with "Nazi Supremacists" and the "Ku Klux Klan"![58]

The spiritual difference between that group and true Biblical Christianity is as clear as the divine contrast between light and darkness! Just a few "minor" examples are:

Since 1866 the "KKK" has taught and evidenced demonic hatred for virtually anyone (primarily Jewish and African) who is not "pale-complexioned" as they are. But the God of true Biblical Christianity evidenced on Calvary's cross unconditional love for all people (John 3:16-18) in perfect balance with His Holy Righteous nature as Judge of the world (John 16:8)!

Thus for over almost a century and a half, the god of that demonic hate-group and his followers have historically perpetrated vigilante terror and murder on countless innocent people, further evidencing their hatred for God and His Sixth Commandment "Thou shalt not kill" (Exodus 20:13). But the God of true Biblical Christianity is the divine author of love, peace and life, offering such to all as "the Way, the Truth and the Life" (John 14:6) - Jesus the "Prince of Peace" (Isaiah 9:6)!

The god of that demonic vigilante hate-group and his followers publicly claim to be "angels of light", though their demonic deeds are usually done in darkness of night behind cowardly disguise. But the lovingly transparent God of Biblical Christianity is the true "LIGHT of the World" (John 8:12), publicly revealing His Holy radiance and offer of redemption to those in bondage to the darkness of sin!

The loving God of true Biblical Christianity divinely lifts up the cross for all to see His beloved Son, who sacrificially died offering redemption by paying the price for the sins of the entire world! But the god of that demonically dark vigilante hate-group and his reprobate followers rebelliously regard Christ's cross as mere worthless refuse to burn.

It's tragically evident today that much of America has indeed sadly forgotten her rich spiritual heritage bestowed by Founders, as even a "democratic" President whose very party-affiliation evidenced he himself had forgotten our Republic (Woodrow Wilson) prophetically warned, "A nation which does not remember what it was yesterday, does not know what it is today nor what it is trying to do; we are trying to do a futile thing if we do not remember where we came from or what we have been about"![59]

This President whether knowingly or not, was indeed applying a Biblical principle in his profound quote, as God knew it was our nature to forget wisdom and instruction. Thus the Bible exhorts "REMEMBER the words of the Lord Jesus" (Acts 20:35)!

God's churches in America must divinely remember His Words, and faithfully rediscover America's Bible-based Christian Republic wisely bestowed by our Founders!

Is it too late? God has obviously not yet rendered ultimate judgment since our beloved nation by His mercy and grace still exists!

But even if America's pastors repent, leading her churches to experience genuine spiritual brokenness and revival to rediscover our Founders' Republic, can even God succeed in national spiritual restoration of our Republic to potentially see a great harvest come to Christ in America in time for His glorious return?

God and our Founders' uncomplicated but profoundly conditional Biblical answer as the final step in their 4-R's REMEDY VISION for America may surprise you!

***

## Chapter Eight

Restoring God in Government!

As previously Biblically emphasized, before God can be RESTORED in our government, He has to be humbly and prayerfully invited back into America's repentant churches ("REVIVAL Awakening Authentic Sheep")!

Remember the officially-documented First Amendment Intent of our Founders – to prohibit a federally-established denomination, but ensure the inclusion of God's principles in government ("REDISCOVERING America's Republic")!

According to God and our Founders, the only way to restore God in government and ensure survival of our Republic is to restore Biblical principles back in government! But the only way to restore His principles in government is for Biblical Christians in His churches to faithfully serve in government! And the only way to reproduce Christians in churches and subsequently in government is through Spirit-led witnessing of our faith to future generations, which America and Founders generally understood for almost two centuries!

To put it simply, when God's Biblically faithful people are restored in government, since God lives in the hearts of His true people His presence is restored to government through them – and when God's presence is restored 114 in government, it follows that His principles are actively restored and thus our Bible-based Christian Republic can be restored!

Or to quote my prophetic God-pleaser pastor's simple way of paraphrasing the great hymn "Onward Christian Soldiers" - "When the people of God in America start being His army again and not just His family by getting out of our bunkers (church pews) and march to spiritual battle behind the cross and banner of Christ, God can even heal America"!

As recently mentioned, this is why our Founders profoundly stated "Providence has given to our people the choice of their rulers, and it is the duty as well as the privilege and interest of our Christian nation to select and prefer Christians for their rulers"! – Founder John Jay.

Supreme Court First Chief-Justice Jay made this then common but now intensely-debated declaration because our Founders passionately understood God's condition in Proverbs 29:2, "When the righteous are in authority the people rejoice, but when the wicked beareth rule the people mourn"!

But amidst the more than half-century long spiritual slumber of many churches and based on the results of recent crucial national elections, the very vocal "ungodly" in today's America largely prioritize prosperity, power and pleasure as their heroes while developing demonic spiritual disdain for "religion", observing God's people and churches as hypocritical meek and weak, silent and no longer relevant!

So how can even God succeed in restoring His principles back in America's government today amidst a "once Christian" nation now largely hostile to Christ and His church, whose only evidenced spiritual priority is asserting that their "god" is most powerful?

This perilous picture prophetically parallels I Kings 18 involving a true prophet of God named Elijah, who felt alone and far out-numbered (I Kings 18:22) against Israel's wicked King Ahab and four hundred fifty false prophets of Baal!

But Elijah took initiative to issue a spiritual challenge (I Kings 18:21-24) to carefully prepare an altar of burnt sacrifice calling out in worship to their respective "gods", and "the God that answereth by FIRE, let him be God" (I Kings 18:24)!

So their prophets "called upon the name of Baal from morning even until noon, but there was no voice, nor any that answered" (I Kings 18:26)! Elijah then "repaired (restored) the altar of the LORD that was broken down" (I Kings 18:30) and even surrounded with a great trench, challenging Ahab's followers to pour twelve barrels of water on it until the trenches overflowed! Then Elijah called out in prayer:

> "Hear me O LORD, that this people may know that thou art the Lord God, and that thou hast turned their heart back again – Then the FIRE of the Lord fell, and consumed the burnt sacrifice – And when all the people saw it , they fell on their faces and said, The LORD, He is God"
> (I Kings 18:37-39)!

Today in America, an ever-growing spiritually lost nation is skeptically watching to see if God's largely dormant churches will divinely manifest the FIRE and omnipotent power of God by publicly and actively standing up for our faith especially against the wicked rulers in government as Elijah did!

116

Years ago a Christian relayed a "convicting humorous" but true account about a government leader who confided to him that a lot of voters were "really upset about a proposed referendum"! The Christian asked "How do you know that many people are so upset"? This official replied, "Because we received six letters and phone calls expressing opposition"!

If a mere half dozen contacts expressing voter outrage can strike fear in elected leaders, imagine what just one Sunday School class or church of actively-involved Christians can do to respectfully but effectively evidence the "fire and fear of God" upon many "politicians" today!

Tragically at least one professing Christian in a church I preached in informed me that he no longer voted because "politics has become so corrupt and wicked that it does not make any difference anymore"! Respectfully but sadly, this type of "silently inactive" Christianity is the primary reason for the spiritual condition of America's churches and government today!

But notice three divinely crucial but often overlooked spiritual (and physical) actions Elijah took in our familiar Biblical account:

First, he boldly seized position on offense, not defense by confronting and actually initiating the challenge to this wicked king!

Even as a little-league football player, we understood the sound philosophy that offense wins games, but defense wins championships! However, even if your defense plays every game perfectly allowing opponents no points, you will still not win any games if your offense pro-

117

duces no points, but at best sentences your team to boring scoreless ties!

For well over a half century in America, even most well-intended Christian efforts to actively combat Satan are usually passive reactions to what the enemy has already aggressively done!

Imagine what will happen in these perilous last days when God's spiritual army in America suddenly goes on offense, spiritually attacking and damaging "the gates of hell" (Matthew 16:18)!

With mere men this is indeed impossible, but "with God all things are possible" (Matthew 19:26)! The prophetic question is, when or will America's churches collectively get tired enough of silently sitting on the "pew-bench" watching our team's earthly losses, to get in the game and start playing aggressive offense and not just passive defense?

Second, Elijah diligently did all he could to repair (restore) the altar from the demonic damage inflicted by the frenetic followers of this false god!

Can America's churches stand before God and claim this today? Though the unrepentant wicked in these perilous days have rendered it difficult to fully restore our Bible-based Republic, imagine what will happen when God's churches start wisely and effectively being His Remedy instead of merely part of the problem by individually and collectively doing all we can to help repair and restore our Founders' bestowed spiritual foundation!

Third, Elijah humbly and faithfully called out in prayer to the God of Israel, humbly beseeching His Omnipotent power to manifest His sovereign Deity to this wicked king's false god and skeptical followers!

If America's churches are ever going to evidence His power to restore God in our Republic, it is only going to happen when we are willing to humble ourselves in prayer to God, begging Him to use our obedient initiative and restorative efforts to manifest His power, so that America's false worshippers of prosperity, power and pleasure may be divinely and inevitably convinced of His Sovereign Deity and come to know Him on a national scale!

Obviously today in America this seems a daunting task, as the primary challenging consequence of her churches' long spiritual sleep impeding this crucial fourth condition for national spiritual restoration remains that a nation once largely known for her Biblical faith has subtly dropped the spiritual baton in passing our faith across the generations, reaping today's ever-growing God-less society and government.

Based on His churches' present rate of witnessing to and winning souls to Christ in America, our beloved Bible-based Christian Republic could conceivably perish from the earth or cease to collectively practice as such! Thus God's churches must surely awaken and restore her passion and involvement in personal evangelism, since every individual soul is eternally priceless to Jesus!

Consider that even today in America, if there were only one hundred million professing church-going Christians in a population of now over three hundred fifteen million (less than thirty-three percent), and if only five percent of Christians annually led one person to Christ with each new convert annually leading another to Jesus, then at a 1.3 percent annual population growth, within just five years America's Republic could be restored as a "majority" Christian nation again!

This obviously reveals the divine value and need for individual personal evangelism and discipleship as God's primary and most effective way to win a lost world to Christ! Sadly during the past half century or more, even this ultra-conservative hypothetical scenario has not yet been closely approached by America's churches, so we must become actively true to His Great Commission (Matthew 28:18-20) to pray, worship, work and witness so that it will before He returns!

But if we hope to see His healing touch upon our nation and our Republic restored as conditionally promised in 2 Chronicles 7:14, it is plainly obvious that His church must also broaden her vision for a great harvest of souls to Christ by restoring God in government, manifesting His omnipotent power as the only true God as we divinely mobilize to publicly stand up for our faith and reclaim right stance in the public arenas!

If our divinely powerful Heavenly Father can stir His churches in America to manifest His omnipotent fire and power to a largely skeptical government and nation, the followers of prosperity, power and pleasure will divinely and inevitably take notice of our God, even as Baal's false prophets did in Elijah's day!

God's beloved children in His "nurturing family of faith" must arise from our "pew bunkers" and start marching as His spiritual army of sacrificial soldiers of the cross to wage spiritual battle against our adversary Satan by witnessing for Christ, but we must also allow God to transform our attitude about involvement in government, not politics!

Since God ordained government to reward the righteous and punish the wicked (Ezra 7:25-27), "politics" is merely Satan's attempted distortion of God's purpose for government by rewarding the wicked and punishing the righteous – sounds like America's headlines today!

The problem is not with God's ordained institution of government, just as the problem is not with His ordained institution of covenant marriage, but the root problem is the spiritual condition of its occupants reaping divine judgment!

Therefore, Christians must become divinely open, receptive and willing to the possibility of God's high calling into government, instead of disdaining this divine possibility due to our distorted perceptions of government as "wicked politics"!

In fact, most Christians today seem to think that the only way to be in the center of God's will is to go into vocational ministry, a calling which if truly from God and obediently heeded in one's life is indeed the highest calling!

But remember God says "Blessed is the nation whose God is the Lord" (Psalm 33:12). For God to be Lord of a nation, He must first be Lord of her churches - and if He is truly Lord of her churches, inevitably His church will faithfully endeavor to crown Him Lord of her nation and government!

In America today, we have increasingly more churches and numbers in ministry than any previous era in history! Yet the spiritual condition of our nation continues to demonically degenerate at perilously unprecedented rates!

This strongly evidences that Satan is likely most content and even ecstatic to passively observe our nation's apparent minimally-impactual glut of growth in ministry, since it is allowing him to maintain and even expand his vast spiritual void of God's faithful people in government!

But if only one woman partially succeeded in removing some of God's Biblical principles from government in the early '60's, imagine what God will do through thousands and even millions of faithful Christians doing all they can do to spiritually assault "the gates of hell" in America by personally winning the lost to Christ and penetrating the walls of wicked politics in this now practicing demonic democracy to meet His conditions for a great harvest of souls!

But even if America does not repent, God's faithful remnant of Ezekiel 3 "watchmen" will Biblically be able to stand in eternity at His Bema Seat with hands unstained by blood for their faithful efforts to redemptively warn the wicked!

Prayerfully Jesus will gloriously return to find in America a repentant and radiantly revived church bride, as evidenced by her righteous rediscovery and faithful labor toward restoring our faithful Founders' Bible-based Christian Republic!

Remember George Mason's prophetic declaration, "As nations cannot be rewarded or punished in the next world, so they must be in this; by an inevitable chain of causes & effects, Providence punishes national sins by national calamities", revealing our Founders' profound understanding as to the earthly temporal limitation of national blessings or cursings?

Unlike nations however, each of us are individually subject to both earthly and eternal judgment ultimately on that day of verdict before God, "As it is appointed unto men once to die, but after this the judgment" (Hebrews 9:27).

But God's loving offer of escape from eternal deception and death is by repentance and faith in truth! Jesus said "I am the way, the TRUTH, and the life: no man cometh unto the Father but by Me" (John 14:6), and offers "Ye shall know the truth, and the truth shall make you free" (John 8:32).

Thus, God's only way for collective nations to be spiritually saved is for each individual citizen to be personally saved from his sin through repentance and faith in His only Son, the Lord Jesus Christ! Thus you can individually help spiritually restore America and her churches by allowing Him to personally redeem and save you from your sin!

Trusting you are not personally willing to risk your eternal fate by passively observing the peril of these last days manifesting before your eyes, to get apocalyptically left behind to face earthly Great Tribulation, separation from God and eternal torment in a place called Hell, which the Bible's loving and redemptive God intended only for the devil and his angels cast out of Heaven, then consider life's most important question!

Suppose Jesus asked you "Why should I let you into heaven"? What would you say to Him? If there is any doubt about your eternal destiny, you can settle it once and for all right now by sincerely praying a childlike but divinely sincere heartfelt prayer such as this:

"Dear Lord, I know I am a sinner and cannot save myself – but thank you for dying on the cross for my sins – I now REPENT of my sin and through FAITH ask You to come into my heart Lord Jesus - forgive my sins and save my soul – I give you my life, make me the person You want me to be through daily prayer, Bible study and faithful worship and service in a Christ-centered, Bible-believing and Bible-preaching church – in JESUS' name I pray, AMEN"!

"He that hath an ear, let him hear" (Revelation 2:7)!
"Come, and let us (spiritually restore)" (Nehemiah 2:17)!
"Even so, come Lord Jesus" (Revelation 22:20)!

Dear loyal American Patriot!

Thank you for wisely investing your valuable time to personally read and apply GRFA's prophetically-rare Divinely-needed book! This 15-year labor of love prayerfully endeavors to redemptively but boldly proclaim the heart of God and America's Founders about our beloved Bible-based Christian Republic's spiritual survival as a nation! Accordingly, I humbly but truthfully testify that the prophetic words contained in this manuscript come from an infinitely-higher source than a mere author toward fulfillment of God and Founders' 4-R's Remedy VISION for America, prayerfully reaping a Great Harvest to Christ for His return!

"We recognize no sovereign but God and no King but Jesus"
- America's Founders
"Where there is NO vision, the people perish"
- Proverbs 29:18
"If My people which are called by my name shall humble themselves and pray, and seek My face and turn (REPENT) from their wicked ways; then will I hear from Heaven, and will forgive their sin and will heal their land"
- 2Chronicles 7:14
"Come, and let us spiritually RESTORE...that we be no more a reproach" - Nehemiah 2:17
"He that hath an ear, let him hear HEAR what the Spirit saith" - Revelation 2:17

As HE and our faithful Founders inspire you to action, I would be Divinely grateful for your faithful recommendation of GOD And FOUNDERS' REMEDY For AMERICA to all within your sphere of influence, both in person and via social media! GRFA would also appreciate your personal review on amazon.com - may God be able to BLESS America!

## BIOGRAPHY

Rev Stephen Forfer, a native of predominantly-Catholic New Orleans, LA was a 1975 alumnus of Jesuit High School and a 1979 graduate of Louisiana State University in Baton Rouge with a Bachelors Degree in Accounting. After 11 years in secular vocation, in 1992 he entered New Orleans Baptist Theological Seminary (NOBTS), graduating in 1995 with a Masters Degree in Pastoral Studies.

He was pastor of Southern Baptist churches in Louisiana and Mississippi, as well as interim-pastor of several others, seeing souls gloriously saved, baptized and discipled in God's Holy Word, the Bible! He was chosen to serve as a member of NOBTS' Presidential-Search Committee that recommended President Charles Kelley, and prior to ministry-call was Chapter-President of Mississippi Right-To-Life (Warren County).

As a six year old boy in 1963, God divinely planted a seed in his life for future salvation and ministry call as he silently observed his beloved mother crying over "some decision about school prayer". When he later asked why she wept, her life-changing response was the seed God would use to help gloriously save him in 1982 and heed God's call to ministry in 1991.

The Founding Evangelist of God's Remedy For America (GRFA) Evangelism Ministry [www.GodsRemedyForAmerica.yolasite.com] since 2000 whose prophetically-rare but Divinely-needed Sermon-series Manuscript published by "Christian News Today" required fifteen years' prayerful preparation is evangelistically dedicated to God's healing and restoration of America's unique spiritual foundation via His

"4-R's" VISION based on 2 Chronicles 7:14 and Nehemiah 2:17.

Stephen is a powerfully prophetic evangelical "Church-Revival" preacher for any having "ear to hear" (Revelation 2:7), as well as an anointed National Speaker for secular organizations, divinely convinced "GRFA" is America's only Biblical hope for a GREAT HARVEST to CHRIST prior to His glorious return!

He is married to the former Doris Landrum of New Orleans since 1985. They have one cherished daughter Emily, a Christian "Home-School" & state-accredited College graduate faithfully serving as a licensed public school Teacher (K-G3).

*TO SCHEDULE GOD'S REMEDY FOR AMERICA EVANGELISM MINISTRY [GRFA] FOR YOUR CHURCH OR ORGANIZATION*

GRFA's powerfully-prophetic Newsletters are received nation-wide as further fulfillment of His's 4-R's Remedy Vision to RESTORE Founders' Bible-based Christian Republic, prayerfully reaping a Great Harvest to Christ in America for His return! To receive complimentary editions of Rev Forfer's newsletters, contact:

Evangelist Stephen G. FORFER
GOD'S REMEDY FOR AMERICA Evangelism Ministry
[GRFA]
GodsRemedyForAmerica.yolasite.com
StephenForfer@gmail.com

# ENDNOTES

1 Strong, James. 2013, "Strong's Greek Definition for #5046. http://www.apostolic- churches.net/bible/strongs/ref/?st-gh=greek&stnm=5046

2 Wikepedia.2013, "George Whitefield".Last modified August 31.Accessed September 3, 2013.http://en.wikipedia.org/wiki/George_Whitefield.

3 Barton, David. 1994, "Keys to Good Government" According To The Founding Fathers (VHS) WallBuilders, Inc. Aledo, TX produced and directed by Tri-Star Pictures.

4 Wikepedia. 2013. "Edict of Milan". Last modified May 27.Accessed September 3, 2013. http://en.wikipedia.org/wiki/Edict _of_Milan.

5Barton, David. 1994, "Keys to Good Government" According To The Founding Fathers (VHS) WallBuilders, Inc. Aledo, TX produced and directed by Tri-Star Pictures.

6 Ibid.

7 Ibid.

8 Jefferson, Thomas. 2004, Accessed September 5, 2013. http://www.monticello.org/site/jefferson/democracy-nothing-more-mob-rule.

9 Franklin, Benjamin. 2013, Accessed September 5, 2013.http://www.americanhistorycentral.com/entry.php?rec=469&view=quotes.

10 Barton, David. 1990, 1992, "America's Godly Heritage" (VHS) WallBuilders, Inc. Aledo, TX

11 Ibid

12 Ibid

13 Ibid

14 Ibid

15 Ibid

16 Ibid

17 Ibid

*18* Darwin, Charles(1859) "The Origin of Species By Means of Natural Selection". (1st Edition) London

*19* Barton, David. 1994, "Keys to Good Government" According To The Founding Fathers (VHS) WallBuilders, Inc. Aledo, TX produced and directed by Tri-Star Pictures.

*20* The Word Out.2013."Political Candidates".Accessed September 9, 2013.http://www.thewordout.net/pages/page.asp?page_id=52073.

*21* Barton, David. 1990, 1992, "America's Godly Heritage" (VHS) WallBuilders, Inc. Aledo, TX

*22* Wikipedia. 2013, "Madalyn Murray OHair.Last modified August 30.Accessed September 9, 2013. http://en.wikipedia.org/wiki/Madalyn_Murray_OHair#American_Atheists.

*23* Wikipedia. 2013. "Roe v. Wade".Last modified August 10.Accessed September 10, 2012.
 http://en.wikipedia.org/wiki/Roe_v._Wade.

*24* Barton, David. 1990, 1992, "America's Godly Heritage" (VHS) WallBuilders, Inc. Aledo, TX

*25* Logan, Jim, "Reclaiming Surrendered Ground", (Chicago: Moody Publishers, 1st Edition, 1995) 38 -42

*26* Barton, David. 2013."Is the U.S. a Christian Nation?"(Debate) Part 1 Barton v Annie Laurie Gaylor Accessed September 10, 2013.http://www.youtube.com/watch?v=CKUqobolSWQ
Part 2 http://www.youtube.com/watch?v=sV_fHE_VuCU

*27* Barton, David. 1990, 1992, "America's Godly Heritage" (VHS) WallBuilders, Inc. Aledo, TX

*28* Barton, David. May 14, 2013, "Noah Webster The Bible".WallBuilders, Inc., Aledo, TX(Historical Documents). Accessed September 12, 2013.http://wallbuilders.com/libissuearticles.asp?id=144363.

*29* Barton, David. May 2008, "John Adams, The Founding Fathers on Jesus, Christianity and the Bible"WallBuilders, Inc., Aledo, TX (Issues/Articles).Accessed September 12,

2013.

http://wallbuilders.com/libissuearticles.asp?id=8755.

*30* Barton, David. 1990, 1992, "America's Godly Heritage" (VHS) WallBuilders, Inc. Aledo, TX

31 Ibid.

*32* Barton, David. May 2008, "Benjamin Rush, The Founding Fathers on Jesus, Christianity and the Bible"WallBuilders, Inc., Aledo, TX (Issues/Articles).Accessed September 12, 2013.

http://wallbuilders.com/libissuearticles.asp?id=8755.

*33* Barton, David. 1990, 1992, "America's Godly Heritage" (VHS) WallBuilders, Inc. Aledo, TX

*34* Barton, David. 1994, "Keys to Good Government" According To The Founding Fathers (VHS) WallBuilders, Inc. Aledo, TX produced and directed by Tri-Star Pictures.

*35* Ibid

*36* Ibid

*37* Ibid

*38* Ibid

*39* Ibid

*40* Barton, David. 1990, 1992, "America's Godly Heritage" (VHS) WallBuilders, Inc. Aledo, TX

*41* Barton, David. 1994, "Keys to Good Government" According To The Founding Fathers (VHS) WallBuilders, Inc. Aledo, TX produced and directed by Tri-Star Pictures.

*42* Ibid.

*43* Ibid.

*44* Barton, David. 1990, 1992, "America's Godly Heritage" (VHS) WallBuilders, Inc. Aledo, TX

*45* USA News First.September 11, 2013."George Washington:Learn Religion of Jesus Christ in Schools". Accessed September 19, 2013.http://www.usanewsfirst.com/2012/09/11/george-washington-learn-religion-Of-jesus-christ-in-schools/#sthash.U8jdbBMJ.dpbs

46 Barton, David. May 2008, "John Witherspoon, The Founding Fathers on Jesus, Christianity and the Bible"Wall-Builders, Inc., Aledo, TX (Issues/Articles).Accessed September 19, 2013. http://wallbuilders.com/libissuearticles. asp?id=8755.

47 Adams, John.Accessed November 1, 2013.http://ushistorysite.com/adams_quotes.php

48 Barton, David. May 2008, "Noah Webster, The Founding Fathers on Jesus, Christianity and the Bible"WallBuilders, Inc., Aledo, TX (Issues/Articles).Accessed September 19, 2013.
http://wallbuilders.com/libissuearticles.asp?id=8755.

49 Barton, David. May 2008, "Thomas Jefferson, The Founding Fathers on Jesus, Christianity and the Bible"WallBuilders, Inc., Aledo, TX (Issues/Articles).Accessed September 19, 2013. http://wallbuilders.com/libissuearticles.asp?id=8755.

50 Barton, David. May 2008, "John Adams, The Founding Fathers on Jesus, Christianity and the Bible"WallBuilders, Inc., Aledo, TX (Issues/Articles).Accessed September 20, 2013.
http://wallbuilders.com/libissuearticles.asp?id=8755.

51 American Minute. "John Marshall, 4th Chief Justice of the Suspreme Court"Accessed September 23, 2013. http://www. americanminute.com/index.php?date=09-24.

52 Barton, David. 1990, 1992, "America's Godly Heritage" (VHS) WallBuilders, Inc. Aledo, TX

53 Wikipedia. 2013 "List of Presidents of the United States" Last modified September 23, 2013. Accessed September 25, 2013.http://en.wikipedia.org/wiki/List_of_Presidents_of_ the_United_ States.

54 Wikipedia. 2013 "Mormonism" Last modified September 24, 2013.Accessed September 25, 2013. http://en.wikipedia. org/wiki/Mormonism.

55 Wikipedia. 2013 "List of Presidents of the United States"

Last modified September 23, 2013. Accessed September 25, 2013.http://en.wikipedia.org/wiki/List_of_Presidents_of_the_United_ States.

*56* Wikipedia. 2013, "Slavery" Last modified September 23, 2013.Accessed September 26, 2013. http://en.wikipedia.org/wiki/Slavery#Modern.

*57* Wikipedia. 2013, "Sodomy Laws in the United States" Last modified September 20, 2013.
 Accessed September 26, 2013. http://en.wikipedia.org/wiki/Sodomy_laws_in_the_United _States#State_laws_prior_to_2003.

*58* Wikipedia. 2013, "Ku Klux Klan" Last modified September 25, 2013.Accessed September 26, 2013. http://en.wikipedia.org/wiki/Ku_Klux_Klan.

*59* Barton, David. 1994, "Keys to Good Government" According To The Founding Fathers (VHS) WallBuilders, Inc. Aledo, TX produced and directed by Tri-Star Pictures.

# Index

# S